Quick & Tasty

75 WONDERFUL RECIPES

FEATURING

MEATS

H.E. Butt Grocery Company

SAN ANTONIO, TX

Quick & Tasty
75 wonderful recipes featuring HEB Fully Cooked Meats
Copyright 2004 by Silverback Books, Inc.

Recipes: Linda Lackey, HEB Culinary Department
Text: Ann Beman, Sandy Szwarc
Editor: Lynda Zuber-Sassi
Photography: Lisa Keenan
Food Styling: Agnes (Pouke) Halpern
Prop Styling: Carol Hacker
Design and Production: Patty Holden

ISBN: 1-930603-68-1

Printed in Singapore

$7.99

Table of Contents

Side Dishes

HEB's Meaty Proposition

Take a moment to think about your family's ideal meal. Maybe it's a casual, outdoor event with slow-smoked barbecued meats, lots of family, homemade side dishes and Chamber of Commerce weather. Maybe it's a formal event with succulent meats that have been cooked to perfection, exotic fruits and vegetables and perfectly behaved children and guests. Or maybe it's as simple as a wholesome meal that the entire family enjoys as they eat it at the same time…without the television taking the place of conversation! The ideal meal means something different to each one of us. But there is a common thread; they are few and far between.

In reality, the daily demands on time are far too great for every meal to be the ultimate occasion. With HEB Fully Cooked meats on hand, however, home-cooks can create awe-inspiring meals—each and every day—with minimal time and effort.

It begs the question. Why offer a *cook*book that features "fully cooked" products? Because HEB Fully Cooked meats are building blocks to quick-yet-fabulous meals that tower over the alternatives—expensive and often unwholesome fast food, or dishes so labor intensive that the harried cook collapses with exhaustion before being able to put anything on the table.

HEB Fully Cooked meats were born of an idea that is about 6 years old. In an effort to respond to you, the consumer, and your need for more convenient foods, HEB challenged its meat department to envision and create meat products that are fast and easy to prepare. In addition, these pre-cooked meats needed to be exceptional in quality and flavor, and available at a fair price. They needed to exemplify meats that are better than most people can cook themselves.

Initially, HEB started with five different Fully Cooked products and has since grown to more than 200—with more to come.

The inspiration to compose a cookbook featuring these meats came straight from the HEB Culinary Department, a team dedicated to providing HEB shoppers with solutions for mealtimes. Their mission is to improvise recipes, share product knowledge, and exchange time-saving tips and general kitchen and cooking "know how." And they carry that mission out with a passion, which they have channeled into this collection of authentic recipes made for Texans by Texans.

As you will discover, the dishes are imaginative, delicious, contemporary, and—best of all—easy. They call for simple ingredients, and yield spectacular results in a short period of time.

We encourage homecooks to take these recipes and make them their own, with slight or grand variations. After all, variety is a crucial ingredient. We hope this book, too, will add spice to your family's lifestyle.

MOLLY KAYE MCADAMS, PH.D.
DIRECTOR OF PRODUCT AND
OWN BRAND DEVELOPMENT,
HEB GROCERY COMPANY

Appetizers
&Snacks

Asian Lettuce Wraps

Preparation Time: 10 minutes
Cooking Time: 10 minutes
Makes 4 servings, 3 wraps each

1 bag (12 ounce) frozen
**H-E-B Fully Cooked®
Beef Crumbles**

½ cup hoisin sauce

½ cup prepared Thai or
Asian-style peanut sauce

½ seedless or hothouse
cucumber, chopped

½ cup shredded carrot

¼ cup torn, fresh mint leaves

12 large Boston, Bibb or
butterhead lettuce leaves

Fresh mint leaves for garnish,
optional

You could say that these delectable lettuce wraps are the Asian answer to tacos. Butterhead lettuce, of which Boston and Bibb are the best-known varieties, features buttery-textured greens that are sweet and succulent. Cradled in the lettuce's small, bowl-shaped leaves, H-E-B's Beef crumbles, Asian sauces, and fresh, crisp vegetables make clever-looking and great-tasting appetizers or snacks.

1. Heat beef crumbles in a 2-quart microwave-safe dish according to package directions.

2. Stir in hoisin sauce and peanut sauce; microwave briefly to heat.

3. Add cucumber, carrots and torn mint leaves, toss gently.

4. Spoon beef mixture, divided evenly, into center of each lettuce leaf to make 12 wraps. Add additional mint leaves for garnish, if desired. Roll up and serve immediately.

Beef Chalupas Compuestas

Preparation Time: 10 minutes
Heating Time: 10 minutes
Makes 8 Chalupas

1 package (12 ounce)
H-E-B Fully Cooked®
Taco Beef Crumbles

1 can (16 ounce) refried beans

8 tostadas or chalupa shells

1 avocado, seeded and peeled
or 8 ounces H-E-B Fresher
Lasting™ Avocado

1 cup salsa picante

⅓ cup regular or light
sour cream

⅓ cup (4 ounces) shredded
colby Jack cheese

Spanish for "boat" or "launch," a chalupa is a crisp corn tortilla formed into a small boat shape. Our chalupas compuestas are composed of H-E-B Fully Cooked® Taco Seasoned Beef Crumbles, frijoles, avocado, and flavorful fixings. When a quick, satisfying snack is being requested from the galley, these hearty bites will keep your crew afloat. Que sabrosas! So delicious.

1. Heat oven to 350°F.

2. Heat beef crumbles in microwave according to package directions. Heat beans on stovetop or in microwave until hot.

3. Place tostadas or chalupa shells on a large baking sheet; heat shells in oven 5 to 10 minutes or until crispy and browned. Mash avocado; season with salt and pepper to taste.

4. To assemble chalupas, spread about 3 tablespoons beans over top of each shell; spread one-eighth beef crumbles over each and drizzle each with 2 tablespoons salsa. Spread with avocado and top with sour cream and cheese. Serve immediately.

7-Layer Taco Dip

Preparation Time: 15 minutes
Makes 12 Servings

1 bag (12 ounce) frozen
H-E-B Fully Cooked®
Taco Beef Crumbles

2 cans (16 ounces each)
refried beans

1 package (16 ounce)
refrigerated H-E-B Fresher
Lasting™ Avocado*

Salt and ground black pepper,
to taste

1 cup refrigerated H-E-B
Fresher Lasting™ Roasted Salsa

16 ounces (2 cups) sour cream

2 cups (8 ounces) shredded
colby Jack cheese

4 green onions with tops,
chopped (about ½ cup)

*or 2 cups mashed avocado

This Tex-Mex appetizer, with its kaleidoscope of savory ingredients, is quick, easy, and delicious. It disappears fast, so if you're making the dip for a party, consider preparing a double batch. Reheat the leftovers and spoon them into warmed tortillas for a flavorful burrito or soft taco. An eighth layer of black olives boosts the appeal even further.

1. Heat beef crumbles in microwave according to package directions.

2. Meanwhile, spread beans over bottom of a 9 x 13-inch pan or 2 to 2½ quart casserole dish. Spread beef crumbles over beans.

3. Mash avocado in a medium bowl; season to taste.

4. Layer avocado, salsa and sour cream over beef. Top with cheese and green onions.

Serve 7-Layer Taco Dip with Tortilla or Corn Chips.

Greek-Style Beef Quesadillas

Preparation Time: 20 minutes
Cooking Time: 10 minutes
Makes 5 Quesadillas

1 bag (12 ounces) frozen **H-E-B Fully Cooked® Beef Fajitas**

½ seedless or hothouse cucumber

½ small red onion, thinly sliced

⅓ cup prepared Greek or balsamic vinaigrette dressing

1 package (5-count) handmade pita flat bread

1 tub (8 ounce) regular or roasted garlic cream cheese spread

4 ounces feta cheese crumbles, Mediterranean-style

½ cup (2 ounces) shredded mozzarella cheese

Plain yogurt, optional, for garnish

Feta makes a zesty addition to many salads and cooked dishes. This time around, the crumbly cured cheese teams with cucumber, balsamic vinaigrette, and pita bread to put a distinctly Greek twist on a classic Tex-Mex appetizer. Creamy yogurt introduces a cool, tangy complement to the warm, spicy quesadillas.

1. Cut cucumber lengthwise in half and then crosswise into very thin slices. Toss cucumber with onion and dressing in a medium bowl; set aside to allow flavors to blend.

2. Heat fajitas in microwave according to package directions. Cut into bite-sized pieces.

3. Split each pita horizontally to form a top and bottom. Lay cut-sides up and spread with cream cheese. Arrange fajitas over 5 halves, divided evenly; sprinkle with feta cheese. Layer cucumber and onion over feta (leftover cucumber mixture may be served with quesadillas). Sprinkle with mozzarella cheese. Top each with remaining pita halves, cut-sides down.

4. Heat 2 medium non-stick skillets over Medium heat. Place 1 quesadilla in each skillet; heat 2 to 3 minutes per side, until bread is toasted and filling is hot. Remove from skillet and heat remaining quesadillas with the same method. Cut into wedges; serve with remaining cucumber mixture and garnish with yogurt, if desired.

Chicken and Spinach Quesadillas

Preparation Time: 15 minutes
Cooking Time: 10 minutes
Makes 4 Servings

1 bag (12 ounce) frozen
H-E-B Fully Cooked®
Chicken Breast Fajitas

½ red onion, sliced

3 ounces Cotija cheese,
crumbled (¾ to 1 cup)

1 tablespoon oil

1 bag (5 or 6 ounce) fresh
baby spinach leaves

Salt and ground black pepper

Non-stick cooking spray

8 Southwestern or plain flour
tortillas (6-inch)

Known as the "Parmesan of Mexico," Cotija cheese is strongly flavored, firm and perfect for grating and crumbling. It adds a lively garnish to common dishes as well as uncommonly delicious ones such as quesadillas, which are quick, super tasty, and ingenious in their versatility. This recipe uses chicken breast fajitas, which like all H-E-B Seasoned and Fully Cooked® meats, are convenient and capture that great Texas flavor. With fresh baby spinach, how could these toasty wedges be anything but stellar?

1. Heat fajitas in microwave according to package directions.

2. Meanwhile, cut onion in half; slice very thinly and cut slices in half. Crumble cheese. Cut fajitas into bite-sized pieces.

3. Heat oil in a large, non-stick skillet over Medium-High heat. Sauté onion 5 minutes or until tender. Stir in spinach; cook 30 to 60 seconds until wilted. Season with salt and pepper to taste; remove to a plate.

4. Return skillet to heat; if dry, spray with non-stick spray. Place 1 tortilla in skillet. Sprinkle with 1 tablespoon cheese; spread one-fourth fajita and one-fourth spinach mixture over cheese. Sprinkle with 1 more tablespoon cheese and top with a second tortilla. Press down gently; spray top of tortilla with non-stick spray. Turn over to brown second side. If skillet gets too hot, reduce heat or remove skillet from burner briefly. Heat about 2 minutes per side or until tortillas brown and cheese melts. Remove from skillet.

5. Repeat step 4 to prepare 3 more quesadillas. Cut into wedges and serve.

Quick 'n Easy Nachos

Preparation Time: 10 minutes
Baking Time: 10 minutes
Makes 4 Servings

1 tub (12 ounce) **H-E-B Fully Cooked® Pork Tamale Filling**

1 small bag (8 to 10 ounce) tortilla chips

1 can (15 ounce) pinto or black beans, rinsed and drained

2 cups (8 ounces) shredded cheddar cheese

Nacho jalapeño slices, optional

Prepared guacamole and sour cream, optional

No doubt, this is a family favorite. It is not only the all-time most requested Mexican-style hors d'oeuvre; it's also a highly popular after-school snack. We even know a couple of collegiate types who crave this concoction of layered beef, beans, and melted cheese for breakfast. Be that as it may, we like it as the promising beginning to equally promising South-of-the-Border-themed festivities. We're also fond of these nachos as a quick and easy meal at the end of a hectic day.

1. Heat oven to 375°F. Drain and rinse beans.

2. Spread tortilla chips over bottom of a large baking sheet with sides.

3. Place tamale filling in a medium bowl; pull apart with 2 forks or with hands to "shred". Arrange over chips. Spread beans over tamale filling.

4. Top with cheddar cheese and nacho jalapeno slices, if desired.

5. Bake 10 to 15 minutes, or until cheese is melted and bubbly.

6. Serve with guacamole & sour cream, if desired.

Tenderloin Canapés with Fruit Salsa

Preparation Time: 25 minutes
Serves 8 to 12 for Appetizers

1 pound **H-E-B Fully Cooked®**
Beef Tenderloin Roast

1 to 2 loaves French baguette,
thinly sliced

Creamy Horseradish Sauce:

4 ounces (½ cup) cream
cheese, softened

¼ cup prepared horseradish

2 tablespoons **each** mayonnaise
and Dijon mustard

Fruit Salsa:

1 mango, seeded, peeled
and diced

2 kiwi fruit, peeled and diced

1 red bell pepper, seeded,
stemmed and diced

½ bunch (3 to 4) green onions
with tops, chopped

1 jalapeño pepper, seeded,
stemmed and minced

¼ cup chopped fresh
cilantro leaves

2 tablespoons fresh squeezed
limejuice

Salt, to taste

This palette of colorful ingredients is a study in contrasts—juicy beef tenderloin vs. crusty French bread; the kiss of cream cheese vs. the bite of horseradish; the sweet/tart juicy flesh of mangoes and kiwis vs. the bittersweet crunch of bell peppers. You'll be amazed at how speedily you can create such tasty works of art, while your guests will marvel at their delicious complexity.

1. Toss fruit salsa ingredients together in a medium bowl. Set aside to stand at room temperature 15 to 30 minutes, if time allows.

2. Blend horseradish sauce ingredients together in a separate medium bowl until smooth and creamy. Set aside.

3. Slice beef as thinly as possible, into slices about ⅛-inch thick. If not serving immediately, stack beef slices and wrap tightly with plastic wrap.

4. To assemble canapés, stack beef slices; cut into quarters. Spread one side of each bread slice with horseradish sauce; lay 2 to 3 slices of beef on each (as much as desired). Top canapés with 1 to 2 teaspoons horseradish sauce, according to taste. Serve tenderloin canapés with fruit salsa.

Tenderloin and Tomato Bruschetta

Preparation Time: 30 minutes
Broiling Time: 5 minutes
Makes 20 to 30 Appetizers

1½ to 2 pounds **H-E-B Fully Cooked® Beef Tenderloin Roast**

4 ounces (1 piece) Parmesan cheese, sliced very thinly

1 loaf French baguette

4 cloves garlic, crushed

¼ cup olive oil

Topping:

1 red tomato, finely chopped

1 yellow tomato, finely chopped

2 tablespoons minced red onion

2 tablespoons finely chopped fresh basil

2 teaspoons red wine vinegar

¼ teaspoon salt

From the Italian bruscare *meaning "to roast over coals," this traditional garlic toast makes an ideal base for our delightful tomato concoction, which is sort of an Italian version of salsa. Their bright colors and fragrant aroma will draw company to these little open-faced beef and tomato sandwiches like bumblebees to orange blossoms. No one will guess how easy they were to prepare.*

1. Cut Parmesan into thin slivers with potato peeler or cheese plane and set aside.

2. Combine topping ingredients in a medium bowl; set aside.

3. Heat oven to Broil; place oven rack 4 to 5 inches from broiler.

4. Slice baguette into ½-inch thick slices; place slices on 2 baking sheets. Crush garlic and blend with olive oil; brush lightly over tops of bread. Broil 1 minute per side or until lightly browned. Remove from oven.

5. Remove tenderloin from package; slice into ¼-inch thick slices. Cut slices in half.

6. Arrange bread slices on baking sheets with oiled sides up. Top each with 1 scant tablespoon tomato mixture, one slice tenderloin and a sliver of Parmesan cheese; top with a very small amount of tomato mixture.

7. Broil 1 to 2 minutes. Serve immediately.

Spicy Beef and Queso Dip

Preparation Time: 5 minutes
Cooking Time: 15 minutes
Makes 12 to 18 Appetizer Servings

1 bag (12 ounce) frozen
H-E-B Fully Cooked®
Taco Beef Crumbles

2 pounds H-E-B Easy
Melt™ Cheese

2 cans (10½ ounces each)
diced tomatoes and
green chilies

How can something with so few ingredients and so few steps be such a mouth-watering treat? The answer is simple with H-E-B's Fully Cooked® beef and Easy Melt™ cheese. With a recipe this quick and easy there's more time to dip your chips into this satisfying starter. For a change of pace, pour this cheesy dip over a platter of tortilla crisps. Ole! Nachos ride again.

1. Place beef crumbles in a 3-quart microwave-safe dish; follow package directions for microwave heating.

2. Meanwhile, cut cheese into 1-inch cubes.

3. Add cheese and diced tomatoes with green chilies to dish with beef crumbles. Cover and microwave on High power 8 to 10 minutes; stir 2 to 3 times during heating, until cheese melts and dip is hot. Serve with your favorite tortilla or corn chips.

Salads
&Soups

Confetti Pasta Salad Enchilado

Preparation Time: 15 minutes
Cooking Time: 10 minutes
Makes 4 to 6 Servings

1 bag (12 ounce) frozen **H-E-B Fully Cooked® Beef Fajitas**

8 ounces uncooked tri-color rotini or fusilli pasta

1 can (16 ounce) black beans

1 can (11 ounce) corn kernels

1 medium red bell pepper, seeds and stem removed

¼ cup finely chopped red onion

4 ounces queso enchilado, shredded

½ cup chopped cilantro leaves

Dressing:

⅓ cup extra virgin olive oil

¼ cup fresh squeezed limejuice

1 teaspoon salt

½ teaspoon ground black pepper

Pasta salads make the best dishes for pot lucks, picnics, or quick and easy dinners. They can be made ahead and won't wilt like lettuce salads. This no-fuss salad has all of our favorite fajita fixin's in a single bowl. Grilled beef fajita strips, beans, corn, onion, cheese and cilantro—it's all in there!

1. Bring 10 cups water to a boil in a 4-quart pot. Cook pasta in boiling water about 10 minutes or until just tender. Drain pasta well.

2. While pasta cooks, heat fajitas according to package directions; cut into bite-sized pieces. Whisk dressing ingredients together in a small bowl.

3. Toss warm pasta and fajitas with dressing in a large bowl; set aside 5 to 10 minutes to allow flavors to blend.

4. Meanwhile, rinse and drain black beans. Drain corn. Chop bell pepper. Chop red onion finely. Shred queso enchilado, including edges with seasoning. Chop cilantro.

5. Toss beans, corn, bell pepper, onion, cheese and cilantro with pasta mixture. Serve at room temperature or refrigerate and serve cold.

Serve Confetti Pasta Salad Enchilado with Hot Tortillas.

Fajita Taco Salad

Preparation Time: 15 minutes
Makes 4 Servings

1 bag (12 ounce) frozen
H-E-B Fully Cooked® Beef
or Chicken Fajitas

1 can (15 ounce) kidney or
black beans, rinsed and drained

1 large tomato, coarsely chopped

1 large avocado, cut into small
wedges

1 cup coarsely crushed tortilla
chips or 4 taco salad shells

1 bag (16 ounce) Garden
Salad blend

1 cup (4 ounces) shredded
Monterey Jack or pepper
Jack cheese

1 can (2¼ ounce) sliced ripe
olives, drained

Dressing:

½ cup sour cream

½ cup salsa picante or H-E-B
Fresher Lasting™ Salsa

Taco salads are loved across the Southwest. Laid back and easy, they're right in-style around these parts. They're usually rather unglamorous mounds of taco fixin's, but we've gussied this one up with fajita meat. It's still just as effortless for you because HEB's marinated the meat and grilled it to perfection, and even sliced it for you.

1. Heat fajitas in microwave according to package directions. Cut into bite-sized pieces

2. Meanwhile, rinse and drain beans. Cut tomato and avocado into wedges. Crush tortilla chips (omit chips if using taco shells).

3. Blend dressing ingredients in a large serving bowl; toss with salad greens, beans, tomato, avocado, cheese and olives.

4. If using taco shells, place one-fourth salad mixture in each shell and top with fajita strips. If shells are not used, toss fajita strips with salad and top with crushed chips. Serve immediately.

Serve Beef Fajita Taco Salad with Green Chili Cornbread.

Asian Slaw with Sweet Chili Chicken

Preparation Time: 15 minutes
Makes 4 Servings

2 pieces frozen **H-E-B Fully Cooked® Sweet Chili Seasoned Chicken Breasts**

4 cups thinly sliced Napa cabbage (about ½ head)

½ seedless or hothouse cucumber, sliced

½ cup (½ bunch) sliced green onions, including tops

2 cups (5 ounces) Matchstix® carrots (julienne-cut)

1½ cups chow mein noodles

¼ to ⅓ cup prepared Asian-style dressing

Ordinary slaws can be pretty boring and are rarely filling enough for a full meal. Sweet-spicy Fully Cooked® chicken makes this one a meal, and the Asian dressing brings everything together deliciously. You make it fun and give it extra crunch with those snappy little straw noodles in a can.

1. Heat chicken breasts according to package directions.

2. Meanwhile, slice cabbage and cucumber as thinly as possible. Slice green onions, including tops.

3. Slice chicken breasts across the grain into thin strips.

4. Toss cabbage, cucumber, onions, carrots and noodles in a large bowl with dressing; lay chicken strips over top. Serve immediately.

Serve Asian Slaw with Sweet Chili Chicken with Hot French Bread.

Ensalada Mexicana con Mango y Queso

Preparation Time: 15 minutes
Cooking Time: 5 minutes
Makes 4 Servings

1 bag (12 ounce) frozen
H-E-B Fully Cooked®
Chicken Breast Fajitas

1 head romaine lettuce, cut or
torn into bite-size pieces

4 red or yellow corn tortillas

¼ cup oil for frying

2 mangoes

¼ cup grated queso Cotija

Dressing:

½ cup prepared Caesar salad
dressing

1 tablespoon grated queso Cotija

2 tablespoons chopped cilantro
leaves

1 tablespoon fresh squeezed
limejuice

It's been said that Tijuana was the birthplace of the Caesar salad in the early 1900s. This recipe may remind you of that great salad. But instead of anchovies in the dressing, queso cotija provides the salty touch, and instead of an egg, prepared mayonnaise helps binds it together. Taking it further down Mexico way, we've added lime, cilantro, and fresh mango. You won't miss the croutons, as crunchy tortilla strips feel right at home.

1. Heat fajitas according to package directions.

2. Meanwhile, whisk dressing ingredients together in a medium bowl and set aside.

3. Cut tortillas into ½-inch wide by 2-inch long strips. Heat oil in a medium skillet over Medium-High heat 3 minutes. Lay strips in oil in a single layer. Fry 2 minutes per side; turn strips carefully with a spatula when turning to second side. Drain on paper towels.

4. Cut each mango lengthwise into thirds; discard center sections with seeds. Cut away peel and discard. Cut mangoes into small wedges.

5. Toss lettuce with dressing in a large shallow bowl. Lay fajita strips, mango wedges and tortilla strips over top. Sprinkle with cheese and serve immediately.

Serve Ensalada Mexicana con Mango y Queso with Hot Bolillos.

Sweet Chili Chicken and Mango Salad

Preparation Time: 20 minutes
Makes 4 to 6 Servings

2 to 3 pieces frozen **H-E-B Fully Cooked® Sweet Chili Seasoned Chicken Breasts**

2 ripe mangoes

½ red onion, sliced into rings

1 bag (12 ounce) Fresh Express® Veggie Lover's Salad Blend

1 bag (6 ounce) Fresh Express® Baby Spinach

¼ cup roasted and salted sunflower kernels

Dressing:

2 tablespoons vegetable oil

2 tablespoons white wine vinegar

2 tablespoons frozen orange juice concentrate

1 tablespoon honey

On a summer day, a shady porch provides a fine spot to dine. Make dinner even more welcome by serving something guaranteed to rejuvenate the most heat-wilted appetites. This main-dish salad is satisfying and refreshing with its sweet golden mangoes, sweet-chili seasoned chicken, orange-honey dressing and crunchy sunflower seeds, all nesting in delicate salad greens.

1. Heat chicken according to package directions. Slice into ¼-inch wide x 2-inch long strips.

2. While chicken heats, cut mangoes lengthwise into thirds. Discard center section with seed. Cut remaining thirds into a "grid" pattern, just to the skin. Turn mango inside out and cut mango cubes from skin. Discard skin. Slice red onion very thinly.

3. Whisk dressing ingredients together in a large bowl. Add greens, mangoes and red onions; toss to coat. Lay chicken strips over top and sprinkle with sunflower kernels. Serve immediately.

Serve Sweet Chili Chicken and Mango Salad with French Rolls.

Chicken, Feta and Pine Nut Salad

Preparation Time: 15 minutes
Makes 4 Servings

2 pieces frozen **H-E-B Fully Cooked® Pesto Seasoned Chicken Breasts**

¼ cup pine nuts, toasted

½ head leaf lettuce, torn into bite-sized pieces

½ seedless or hothouse cucumber, sliced

3 small roma tomatoes

⅓ cup coarsely chopped pitted kalamata olives

1 bag (5 ounce) Spring Mix Salad Blend

4 ounces (1 cup) crumbled feta cheese

⅓ cup French vinaigrette dressing

Everyone needs a blueprint salad recipe, you know, a great basic floor plan that invites you to customize the trimmings to your tastes. This one is a terrific all-occasion salad, but you can make it your own by substituting any sharp cheese, lettuce assortment, toasted nuts, and dressing you may love. Whatever you add, H-E-B will supply the Fully Cooked® meat that lets you have a meal on the table in just minutes.

1. Heat chicken breasts according to package directions.

2. Meanwhile, toast pine nuts in a small skillet over Medium heat 3 to 4 minutes, stirring often. Watch carefully to prevent burning. Set aside to cool.

3. Wash and dry leaf lettuce. Tear into bite-sized pieces. Slice cucumber in half lengthwise and then into ¼-inch thick slices. Coarsely chop tomatoes and olives.

4. Toss cucumber, tomatoes and olives with dressing in a large salad bowl; set aside. Cut chicken crosswise into bite-sized pieces.

5. Place lettuce and spring mix in bowl with vegetables; toss to coat. Top salad with chicken, pine nuts and feta cheese. Serve immediately.

Serve Chicken, Feta and Pine Nut Salad with Pesto French Bread.

Pesto French Bread: Heat broiler. Split a loaf of French bread or baguette horizontally. Spread cut sides with refrigerated prepared pesto sauce. Sprinkle with Parmesan cheese. Toast 1 to 2 minutes under broiler. Cut into 2-inch sections and serve while hot.

Mediterranean Pasta and Chicken Salad

Preparation Time: 15 minutes
Cooking Time: 10 minutes
Makes 4 to 6 Servings

2 to 3 pieces frozen **H-E-B Fully Cooked® Italian Seasoned Chicken Breasts**

12 ounces penne rigate pasta

1 bunch fresh asparagus (about 1 pound)

12 to 16 ounces cherry or grape tomatoes

⅔ cup chopped fresh basil

½ cup coarsely chopped pitted kalamata olives

4 ounces (1 cup) crumbled feta or ½ cup shredded Parmesan cheese

Dressing:

¼ cup fresh-squeezed lemon juice

¼ cup balsamic vinegar

¼ cup extra virgin olive oil

1 teaspoon **each** salt and pepper

Summertime is the best time for salad meals that don't require slaving over a hot stove. You'll turn to this recipe again and again whenever you need to bring a dish to a picnic or simply want to celebrate the fresh produce that's so plentiful in Texas. Feel free to ad lib and substitute other seasonal vegetables, such as broccoli instead of asparagus. Or, a variety of juicy-ripe, colored tomatoes can add fun.

1. Bring 4 quarts water to a boil in a 6-quart pot to cook pasta.

2. Meanwhile, heat chicken in microwave according to package directions. Break or cut tough ends from asparagus and discard. Cut asparagus diagonally into 1-inch pieces.

3. Cook pasta in boiling water 8 minutes; add asparagus and boil 1 to 2 more minutes or until asparagus is crisp-tender and pasta is tender yet firm. Drain well.

4. While pasta cooks, cut chicken into 1-inch pieces. Cut tomatoes in half. Chop basil and olives. Whisk dressing ingredients together in a large bowl.

5. Toss warm pasta and asparagus in dressing to coat. Add chicken, tomatoes, basil, olives and cheese; stir gently to combine. Serve salad warm or chilled.

Serve Mediterranean Pasta and Chicken Salad with Toasted Pita Bread.

Bombay Chicken Salad

Preparation Time: 15 minutes
Makes 4 to 6 Servings

2 to 3 pieces frozen **H-E-B Fully Cooked® Seasoned Chicken Breasts**

½ cup slivered almonds, toasted

2 medium apples

1 cup celery, finely chopped (2 large stalks)

⅓ cup chopped green onions (3 to 4)

¼ cup dried currants

Boston or romaine lettuce leaves

Shredded coconut, optional

Dressing:

⅓ cup mayonnaise, regular or reduced-fat

¼ cup prepared mango chutney

2 teaspoons lemon juice

2 teaspoons curry powder

½ teaspoon **each** salt and pepper

The sweet-spiciness of Waldorf salads has been popular since the 1890s. It's time to spice things up! We've given this version an exotic flair with exciting flavors from East India. The cuisine is loved for its curry powders: freshly ground blends of dozens of spices, herbs and seeds—coriander seeds, turmeric, cloves, fennel, fenugreek seeds, peppercorns, cinnamon, cumin, chiles. No two curry powders are the same. Not all are hot, either, but if you like fire look for those labeled "Madras."

1. Heat chicken breasts according to package directions. Dice chicken into ½-inch cubes.

2. Meanwhile, toast almonds in a skillet over Medium heat 2 to 3 minutes, stirring often, until golden; set aside. Blend dressing ingredients in a small bowl and set aside

3. Cut unpeeled apples in half; remove core and seeds. Chop apple and celery finely. Chop green onions. Toss chicken, apple, celery, green onions and currants in a large bowl. Add dressing and toss to coat

4. Arrange lettuce leaves on individual plates or a platter. Spoon salad onto lettuce leaves; top with almonds and sprinkle with coconut, if desired.

Serve Bombay Chicken Salad over Lettuce with Red Grapes and Assorted Crackers.

Italian Meatball Soup

Preparation Time: 5 minutes
Cooking Time: 25 minutes
Makes 4 to 6 Servings

1 bag (16 ounce) frozen
H-E-B Fully Cooked®
Italian Meatballs

2 medium carrots, thinly sliced

1 large onion, chopped

1 medium zucchini squash

1 tablespoon olive oil

2 cans (15 ounces each)
cannellini or white beans,
undrained

1 can (14½ ounce) Italian-style
stewed tomatoes

1 can (14½ ounce) beef broth

½ cup chopped fresh basil
leaves

1 teaspoon **each** salt and pepper

Home-style soups are the repositories of our family's collective memory. All of us can recall our family sitting down to supper of a favorite soup made by our Mom or Grandma. It's fun to have easy, creative soup recipes at your fingertips if the weather turns chilly or it's just a good day for soup. This one's especially loveable as the Italian meatballs add a delicious touch your entire family will love…and long remember.

1. Peel carrots and slice thinly. Chop onion. Cut ends from zucchini and discard. Cut zucchini in half, lengthwise, and then into thin slices.

2. Heat oil in a 4-quart saucepan over Medium-High heat. Sauté carrots and onion 5 minutes. Add zucchini, beans, tomatoes, beef broth and frozen meatballs. Stir and bring to a boil.

3. Cover pot, reduce heat to Medium-Low and simmer 15 minutes, stirring occasionally.

4. Meanwhile, chop basil. Stir basil, salt and pepper into soup and cook 2 more minutes. Serve while hot.

Serve Italian Meatball Soup garnished with shredded Parmesan, if desired, and Hot Garlic Bread.

Toasted Corn and Chicken Soup

Preparation Time: 10 minutes
Cooking Time: 15 minutes
Makes 4 to 6 Servings

1 tub (12 ounce) **H-E-B Fully Cooked® Seasoned Shredded Chicken**

8 ounces queso Cotija, crumbled (about 2 cups)

1 onion, chopped

1 cup finely chopped carrot

4 cloves garlic, minced

1 tablespoon oil

2 cups fresh or frozen corn kernels

2 cans (14½ ounces each) or 3½ cups regular or low-sodium chicken broth

1 cup chopped fresh tomatoes

½ cup chopped cilantro leaves

Optional Garnishes: lime wedges, chopped green onions and Crema Mexicana

Sopas (Spanish for "soups") are a staple of all Tex-Mex cooks. They feed a large family, always taste great, yet are the most forgiving of dishes, letting us throw in most anything and aren't fussy about timing. This light, healthful soup is also a delicious way to eat your vegetables. It will remind you of traditional tortilla soups. In fact, feel free to sprinkle in 4 corn tortillas, cut into thin strips and toasted or fried crispy. If you want to spice things up, toss in a handful of roasted and peeled green chile!

1. Crumble queso cotija and set aside. Chop onion and carrot. Mince garlic.

2. Heat oil in a 4-quart pot over Medium-High heat. Sauté onion and carrot 5 minutes or until onion begins to soften.

3. Stir in garlic and corn; cook 3 to 5 minutes longer or until corn kernels just begin to brown; stir and continue to cook vegetables 5 to 7 minutes longer; stir only when pieces on bottom begin to brown.

4. Add chicken broth and bring to a boil. Add shredded chicken; stir occasionally until heated. Season to taste.

5. Ladle soup into bowls; top with crumbled cotija, tomatoes and cilantro. Serve with lime wedges, chopped green onions and Crema Mexicana, as desired.

Serve Toasted Corn & Chicken Soup with Hot Bolillos.

Sandwiches
&Burgers

Italian Meatball Subs

Preparation Time: 15 minutes
Heating Time: 5 minutes
Makes 4 to 6 Servings

1 bag (16 ounce) frozen
H-E-B Fully Cooked®
Italian Meatballs

4 white or wheat submarine
rolls

16 ounces (2 cups) prepared
pasta or pizza sauce

1 medium green or red bell
pepper

1 bunch green onions with
tops, sliced

½ cup shredded mozzarella
cheese

Submarine sandwiches are "heroes" with just about everyone. These hot ones are stuffed with everything that makes pizza and spaghetti & meatballs two of our favorite foods: a great sauce, melted cheese and hearty Italian meatballs.

1. Heat oven to Broil.

2. Meanwhile, place meatballs in a 2-quart microwave-safe dish; add pasta sauce and heat in microwave according to package directions.

3. Remove seeds and stem from pepper; cut into thin slices. Slice onions.

4. Split rolls; leave one side attached, like a hinge. Open rolls out and place on a large baking sheet, cut-sides down. Toast under broiler 1 to 2 minutes or until lightly browned.

5. Remove from oven and turn rolls cut-sides up. Place meatballs over bottom halves of rolls, evenly divided; arrange pepper strips and onions over top halves. Spoon sauce over meatballs. Top pepper strips and onions with cheese.

6. Place under broiler 1 to 2 minutes or until cheese melts. Close sandwiches and serve immediately.

Serve Italian Meatball Subs with a Tossed Italian Salad.

The Westerner Steak Sandwich

Preparation Time: 10 minutes
Cooking Time: 6 minutes
Makes 4 Servings

4 frozen **H-E-B Fully Cooked®**
Chicken Fried Steaks

1 red or green bell pepper,
seeds and stem removed

4 white or wheat submarine
rolls

1 cup refrigerated H-E-B
Good to Go!® Roasted Salsa
Ranch Dip

Green or red leaf lettuce

Who doesn't love chicken fried steak? But, few of us love all the work of pounding out the meat, and the mess and greasy splatter of dipping it in batter and frying it. This Texas ranch favorite is now easier than ever. H-E-B's Fully Cooked® chicken fries emerge from our microwaves ready to tuck inside hearty rolls and frost with a zesty roasted salsa ranch dip for unbeatable sandwiches.

1. Heat oven to Broil.

2. Meanwhile, heat steaks in microwave according to package directions. Cut bell pepper into thin strips after removal of seeds and stem.

3. Split rolls horizontally; leave one side attached, like a hinge. Open rolls out and place on a large baking sheet, cut-sides down. Toast under broiler 1 to 2 minutes per side or until lightly browned.

4. Spread cut sides of rolls with Salsa Ranch dip, 2 tablespoons per side. Place steaks, pepper strips and lettuce over bottom halves of rolls. Close sandwiches and serve immediately.

Serve The Westerner Steak Sandwich with Corn Chips and Fresh Relishes of Green Onions, Radishes, Carrot and Celery Sticks.

Texas-Style Philly Beef Steak Sandwich

Preparation Time: 10 minutes
Heating Time: 15 minutes
Makes 4 to 6 Servings

1 bag (16 ounce) **H-E-B Fully Cooked® Sliced Philly Beef Steak**

1 loaf French bread or Pan Frances (not baguette)

¾ cup (6 ounces) softened or spreadable cream cheese

⅓ cup sour cream

¼ cup finely chopped fresh or canned jalapeño peppers

½ cup refrigerated H-E-B Fresher Lasting™ Salsa

1½ cups (6 ounces) shredded Monterey Jack cheese

Leave it to a hot-dog vendor to invent another winning sandwich! The genius behind the beloved Philadelphia cheese steak sandwich simply grilled up stacks of thinly sliced beef and onions then tucked it all inside a soft Italian roll. Pretty soon cheese was added to melt delectably and create Philadelphia's most famous sandwich since the Great Depression. Not to be undone, H-E-B makes it possible for Texans to create their own renditions, adding the obligatory fire, of course! Here's an open-face sandwich version with a toasted cheese topping.

1. Heat oven to Broil. Remove pouches from Philly Beef Steak bag. Heat both pouches in microwave according to package directions.

2. Meanwhile, cut bread loaf horizontally; place halves on a baking sheet, cut-sides down. Place under broiler 2 minutes or until lightly toasted. Remove from oven; turn cut-sides up.

3. Combine cream cheese, sour cream and peppers; spread evenly over cut sides of bread.

4. Arrange beef over both halves and drizzle with salsa. Sprinkle evenly with cheese.

5. Place under boiler about 2 minutes or until cheese melts and begins to brown. Cut each half into 2 or 3 portions and serve immediately.

Serve Texas-Style Philly Beef Steak Sandwich with Black Beans with Tomato and Avocado Wedges Served over Lettuce Leaves.

Chicken and Mushroom Sandwich on Ciabatta

Preparation Time: 5 minutes
Cooking Time: 20 minutes
Makes 4 Servings

2 to 3 pieces frozen **H-E-B Fully Cooked® Italian Seasoned Chicken Breasts**

1 medium sweet onion, sliced

4 to 6 ounces sliced fresh babybella mushrooms

2 tablespoons butter

½ cup dry Marsala wine

½ teaspoon ground black pepper

4 ounces fontina cheese, thinly sliced

1 loaf ciabatta bread

Ciabatta is Old World rustic bread with huge holes and amorphous shape that looks like a giant bathroom slipper. Because of its shape, it was christened "ciabatta" or "slipper bread" by a northern Italian baker in the mid-1900s and has since become the national bread of Italy. It's a chewy, light bread, similar to focaccia in flavor, and best baked in a wood-burning hearth or pizza oven so that it develops its characteristic textures. It makes especially light and earthy-tasting gourmet sandwiches.

1. Heat oven to Broil. Microwave chicken according to package directions. Cut chicken crosswise into thin slices.

2. Meanwhile, slice onion. Melt butter in a large skillet over Medium-High heat. Sauté onion and mushrooms 7 to 9 minutes or until tender.

3. Add chicken strips and Marsala to skillet with mushrooms and onion. Add pepper; cook and stir 3 to 5 minutes or until wine is almost evaporated. Remove skillet from heat.

4. Split ciabatta bread horizontally. Toast lightly under broiler, about 1 to 2 minutes per side. Spoon chicken and vegetable mixture over bottom half of bread loaf; top with cheese slices. Return to broiler briefly to melt cheese, if desired. Place top half over bottom; press gently. Cut into 4 portions and serve while hot.

Serve Chicken & Mushroom Sandwich on Ciabatta with a Caesar Salad.

Popcorn Chicken Pita Wraps

Preparation Time: 10 minutes
Heating Time: 12 to 16 minutes
Makes 6 Wraps

12 ounces (½ bag) frozen
H-E-B Fully Cooked®
Breaded or Spicy Breaded
Popcorn Chicken

2 cups shredded lettuce

1 cup diced tomatoes

6 pieces handmade pita
flat bread

½ cup ranch salad dressing

Tuck popcorn chicken nuggets into snug little pita bundles and you're good to go. These make great meals on the run or for transporting— even if you're only going as far as your sofa to watch a movie or the big game.

1. Heat oven to 425°F. Line a large baking sheet with aluminum foil for easy clean up.

2. Place 12 ounces of chicken onto foil-lined sheet in a single layer. Heat in oven 6 to 8 minutes or until tops of chicken are light golden.

3. Remove from oven; scoop pieces up with a spatula and turn chicken to second side. Return to oven and heat 6 to 8 minutes longer or until chicken is golden brown and crispy.

4. Meanwhile, slice lettuce thinly to "shred." Cut tomatoes into ½-inch dice. Heat a medium skillet over Medium-High heat; heat each pita 1 to 2 minutes per side, turning as needed. Wrap in a towel to keep warm.

5. Spread ranch dressing over top sides of pita bread. Place chicken down center of each, divided evenly. Top with lettuce and tomatoes. Close pita, taco-style, and eat while hot.

Serve Popcorn Chicken Pita Wraps with Red and Green Seedless Grapes.

Breaded Chicken Marinara Sandwiches

Preparation Time: 15 minutes
Broiling Time: 5 minutes
Makes 4 Servings

4 pieces frozen **H-E-B Fully Cooked® Chicken Fried Chicken Breasts**

1 package (2-count) French bread sticks

1 green bell pepper, seeds and stem removed

½ cup prepared marinara sauce

4 slices provolone cheese

4 teaspoons grated Parmesan cheese

1 can (2¼ ounce) sliced ripe olives, drained

Hot sandwiches that taste like pizza are sure hits with all ages. To make these, simply sandwich meaty chicken fried chicken breasts between melted provolone-topped bread pizzas. Extra marinara sauce makes these even more finger lickin' good.

1. Heat oven to Broil. Heat chicken in microwave according to package directions.

2. Meanwhile, cut each bread loaf in half and then split each horizontally. Cut bell pepper into ¼-inch thick rings. Place bread halves on a baking sheet, cut-sides down. Heat under broiler about 2 minutes or until lightly toasted.

3. Remove from oven and turn cut-sides up. Spread 2 tablespoons marinara sauce over each bottom half; sprinkle with 1 teaspoon Parmesan. Arrange bell pepper rings, olives and 1 provolone slice over each top half.

4. Return bread to broiler about 2 minutes or until cheese melts. Remove from oven. Place chicken in between top and bottom halves. Heat additional sauce for dipping sandwiches, if desired.

Serve Breaded Chicken Marinara Sandwiches with a Tossed Italian Salad.

Aloha Burgers

Preparation Time: 5 minutes
Heating Time: 5 to 10 minutes
Makes 4 Servings

4 frozen **H-E-B Fully Cooked®**
Thick 'n Tasty Cheeseburgers

1 package (3.5 ounce) pizza-style Canadian bacon

4 hamburger buns or Kaiser rolls

½ cup honey barbecue sauce

1 can (8 ounce) pineapple slices, drained

Boston, Bibb or leaf lettuce leaves

Red onion slices, optional

The first thing that comes to mind when most mainlanders think Hawaiian cuisine is "luau." At this celebratory outdoor feast, a Kalua pig is traditionally slow-cooked in an underground pit oven call an "imu." And, of course our Nation's tropical state is our largest pineapple producer. So, anytime ham and pineapple come together, it's Aloha!

1. Mircowave cheeseburgers according to package directions. Place Canadian bacon slices over burgers; cover with a paper towel and heat 20 to 30 seconds longer in the microwave.

2. Split buns or rolls; toast or heat briefly in microwave.

3. Spread barbecue sauce over buns. Place cheeseburger, pineapple slice and lettuce in between buns. Add red onion slices, if desired. Serve while hot.

Serve Aloha Burgers with Cole Slaw.

Blue Cheese and Apple Burgers

Preparation Time: 15 minutes
Grilling Time: 10 minutes
Makes 4 Servings

4 frozen **H-E-B Fully Cooked®**
Thick 'n Tasty Burgers

1 tart red apple

4 ounces blue cheese, sliced

4 Kaiser rolls or hamburger
buns

½ cup honey mustard

Leaf or romaine lettuce leaves

Red onion slices, optional

Even America's favorite burgers on the grill can get boring after awhile. This amazing burger, topped with sweet-tart apples, creamy blue cheese, and honey mustard, is guaranteed to have your guests bragging about your creativity. And when you start with H-E-B's Fully Cooked® Burgers, you're happy to eliminate the grease and fuss.

1. Heat charcoal 30 minutes until covered with a light layer of gray ash or heat gas grill on High 10 minutes with lid closed.

2. Meanwhile, core apple and trim ends. Cut apple crosswise into 4 slices. Slice cheese as thinly as possible. Split Kaiser rolls or buns.

3. Place frozen burgers directly on grill grate 4 inches above Medium heat (hold palm just above grate; if heat causes you to pull away in 4 seconds, heat is 375°F grill surface temperature and ideal for Medium cooking). Heat burgers 5 minutes per side; place cheese slices on burgers after turning to second side. Place apples on cooking grate; grill 2 to 3 minutes per side. Toast bread around perimeter of grill.

4. Spread mustard over cut-sides of buns, 1 tablespoon per side. Place burgers, apple slices and lettuce leaves in between buns; add sliced onion, if desired. Serve immediately.

Serve Blue Cheese Burgers with Cole Slaw and Your Favorite Chips.

Pizza

Deep Dish Pizza

Preparation Time: 10 to 20 minutes
Cooking Time: 20 minutes
Makes 4 to 6 Servings

1 bag (12 ounce) frozen
**H-E-B Fully Cooked®
Italian Beef Crumbles**

1 box (31.85 ounce) Chef
Boyardee® Pizza Kit (kit
includes marinara sauce
and Parmesan cheese)

1 tablespoon oil (for pizza
kit directions)

8 ounces (2 cups) shredded
mozzarella or pizza-blend
cheese

1 red or green bell pepper,
seeded and cut into rings

1 can (2¼ ounce) chopped
black olives, drained

1 cup chopped green onions,
including tops (1 bunch)

Made popular in Chicago, deep-dish pizzas let you pile on as many toppings as you dare. Be sure to pat out the thick crust up the sides of the dish to help hold the abundant fillings. Remember deep-dish pizzas are full-meal deals—too substantial for eating out of hand. So serve with forks!

1. Heat oven to 425°F. Heat beef crumbles in microwave according to package directions.

2. Meanwhile, prepare crust from pizza kit according to package directions; let dough stand 5 to 20 minutes. Cut bell pepper and onions while dough stands.

3. Spread dough in bottom of a greased 9 x 13-inch baking dish. Spread 1 cup marinara sauce (from kit) over dough; sprinkle with 1 cup shredded mozzarella. Spread all the beef crumbles over cheese. Layer with remaining marinara sauce, 1 cup mozzarella and Parmesan cheese from pizza kit; arrange pepper rings, olives and green onions over top.

4. Bake 18 to 20 minutes, or until crust is browned and cheese is bubbly. Remove from oven; let stand 5 minutes. Cut into squares and serve while hot.

Serve Deep Dish Pizza with a Tossed Caesar Salad.

BBQ Brisket Pizzas

Preparation Time: 15 minutes
Cooking Time: 15 to 20 minutes
Makes 2 Pizzas

1 package (16 ounce) **H-E-B Fully Cooked® Sliced Beef Brisket with BBQ Sauce**

2 Boboli® thin pizza crusts (10 ounces each)

½ to ¾ cup barbecue sauce

2 cups (8 ounces) shredded Monterey Jack cheese

½ cup chopped red onion

½ cup chopped dill pickle

In Texas, barbecue is serious business, but aficionados agree it means beef, and the brisket is king. When you start with H-E-B's sliced brisket with bbq sauce, this pizza is not only perfect for lovers of Texas-style barbecue, but its fast and easy, too.

1. Heat oven to 450°F. Place 2 oven racks in bottom half of oven. Place crusts on baking sheets or round pizza pans.

2. Pour sauce from brisket package into a 1-cup measuring cup. Add additional sauce to make 1 cup; stir to combine.

3. Chop brisket slices coarsely.

4. Spread ½ cup sauce on each pizza crust. Arrange brisket over sauce (about 1 cup beef on each pizza.) Sprinkle cheese, onion and pickle evenly over pizzas.

5. Bake 15 to 20 minutes, or until cheese melts and begins to brown. Rotate pans on oven racks halfway through baking, if necessary, to ensure even browning. Let stand 5 minutes; cut into slices and serve.

Serve BBQ Brisket Pizzas with a Tossed Green Salad with Ranch Dressing.

Shredded Beef and Black Bean Pizzas

Preparation Time: 10 minutes
Cooking Time: 15 minutes
Makes 2 Pizzas

1 tub (12 ounce) **H-E-B Fully Cooked® Seasoned Shredded Beef**

2 Boboli® thin pizza crusts (10 ounces each)

1½ cups salsa picante

4 cups (16 ounces) shredded colby Jack cheese, divided

1 can (16 ounce) black beans, rinsed and drained

1 can (4 ounce) whole green chilies

Crema Mexicana, optional, for garnish

Pizzas are great fun and easy to make because, in a pinch, most anything can be included or exchanged. So if your pantry is missing something, simply omit it and use this recipe as inspiration. You can exchange red or green chile sauce for the salsa, a favorite white cheese or cheese combination for the Jack, and chipotles en adobo for the green chile. You can also add olives, cilantro, or red onion, if you like.

1. Heat oven to 450°F. Place 2 oven racks in bottom half of oven. Place crusts on baking sheets or round pizza pans.

2. Spread ¾ cup salsa over each pizza crust; sprinkle each with 1 cup cheese.

3. Pull beef shreds apart and layer evenly over cheese. Spread beans over beef.

4. Sprinkle 1 cup cheese over each pizza. Cut chilies into thin strips; lay over tops of pizzas.

5. Bake 15 to 20 minutes, or until cheese melts and begins to brown. Rotate pizzas on oven racks halfway through baking, if necessary, to ensure even browning.

6. Remove from oven and let stand 5 minutes. Cut into slices and serve; garnish with Crema Mexicana, if desired.

Serve Shredded Beef and Black Bean Pizzas with Honeydew and Cantaloupe Wedges.

Chicken Pesto Pita Pizzas

Preparation Time: 15 minutes
Cooking Time: 15 to 20 minutes
Makes 6 Pita Pizzas

1 bag (12 ounce) frozen
H-E-B Fully Cooked®
Chicken Breast Fajitas

6 handmade pita flat breads

⅔ cup regular or reduced
fat mayonnaise

2 tablespoons bottled basil
pesto

1 can (14 ounce) quartered
artichoke hearts, drained

1 jar or can (6 ounce) sliced
mushrooms, drained

1 small red bell pepper,
seeds and stem removed

2 cups shredded four cheese
pizza blend

The world's flat breads are becoming increasingly available to us, crossing not just oceans and borders, but culinary traditions as well. In this fusion pizza, we use the traditional-style pita breads from Greece and Turkey as the foundation. These pitas aren't the pocket bread we usually think of, rather, Greek pitas are thick, soft and chewy yeast-raised flat breads used to wrap foods. The fusion is complete with H-E-B chicken fajita strips, Italian pesto, and Mediterranean vegetables and cheese. It all works in perfect unity.

1. Heat oven to 450°F. Place 2 oven racks in bottom half of oven. Line 2 large baking sheets with foil. Lay 3 pita shells on each baking sheet.

2. Microwave fajitas according to package directions. Cut into bite-sized pieces.

3. Meanwhile, combine mayonnaise with pesto; spread evenly over tops of pita bread, about 2 tablespoons on each.

4. Layer chicken, artichoke hearts and mushrooms over pesto, divided evenly. Cut pepper into thin strips; lay strips over tops and sprinkle ⅓ cup cheese over each pita "pizza".

5. Bake 15 to 20 minutes, or until cheese bubbles and begins to brown. Rotate pans on oven racks halfway through baking, if necessary, to ensure even browning. Let stand 5 minutes, cut into slices and serve.

Serve Chicken Pesto Pita Pizzas with Red and Green Seedless Grapes.

Chicken Alfredo Pizzas

Preparation Time: 10 minutes
Baking Time: 15 minutes
Makes 2 Pizzas

1 bag (12 ounce) frozen
H-E-B Fully Cooked®
Chicken Breast Fajitas

2 Boboli® thin pizza crusts
(10 ounces each)

2 roma tomatoes, diced

1½ cups prepared Alfredo sauce

2 cups (8 ounces) shredded
mozzarella cheese

1 can (8 ounce) mushroom
stems and pieces, drained

¼ cup grated Parmesan cheese

Chopped fresh basil leaves,
optional

Alfredo sauce is one of the most decadent sauces imaginable, made of butter, heavy cream and Parmesan. When tossed alone with pasta, it can be too heavy for most of us. But as a pizza sauce it's perfect! As you'll taste in this sophisticated pizza, it adds just the right touch of heavenly rich flavors to simple meats and vegetable toppings.

1. Heat oven to 450°F. Place 2 oven racks in bottom half of oven. Place crusts on baking sheets or round pizza pans.

2. Heat chicken in microwave according to package directions. Cut chicken into bite-sized pieces. Dice tomatoes.

3. Spread ¾ cup Alfredo sauce over each pizza crust. Sprinkle each with 1 cup mozzarella cheese. Layer chicken, mushrooms and diced tomatoes over sauce and cheese. Top with grated Parmesan.

4. Bake 15 to 20 minutes, or until cheese bubbles and begins to brown. Rotate pizzas on oven racks halfway through baking, if necessary, to ensure even browning. Let stand 5 minutes; cut into slices and serve. Sprinkle tops with fresh chopped basil, if desired.

Serve Chicken Alfredo Pizzas with a Tossed Italian Salad.

Barbecue Chicken Pizzas

Preparation Time: 10 minutes
Baking Time: 15 minutes
Makes 2 Pizzas

1 tub (12 ounce) **H-E-B**
Fully Cooked® Seasoned
Shredded Chicken

2 Boboli® thin pizza crusts
(10 ounces each)

1½ cups fire-roasted
barbecue sauce

1 can (8 ounce) pineapple
tidbits, drained

½ cup chopped red onion

8 ounces (2 cups) shredded
mozzarella cheese

Most Texas barbecue pit-meisters know a touch of sweet brings out the best in their sopping sauces. While most of us have a different favorite barbecue sauce, those imparted with smoke usually rank near the top. So, when H-E-B's chefs cooked up this barbecue pizza recipe, you can bet they put a little sweet with a little fire and came up with the best barbecue pizza recipe you'll ever taste.

1. Heat oven to 450°F. Place 2 oven racks in bottom half of oven. Place crusts on baking sheets or round pizza pans.

2. Heat chicken in microwave according to package directions. Pull apart with 2 forks to "shred."

3. Spread ¾ cup barbecue sauce over each crust. Layer chicken, pineapple and onion over sauce on both pizzas. Sprinkle with cheese.

4. Bake 15 to 20 minutes, or until cheese bubbles and begins to brown. Rotate pizzas on oven racks halfway through baking, if necessary, to ensure even browning. Let stand 5 minutes; cut into slices and serve.

Serve Barbecue Chicken Pizzas with Coleslaw and Baked Beans.

Main Dishes

BBQ Beef and Biscuit Casserole

Preparation Time: 10 minutes
Cooking Time: 22 minutes
Makes 4 to 6 Servings

1 tub (16 ounce) **H-E-B Fully Cooked® Shredded Beef Brisket with BBQ Sauce**

Non-stick cooking spray

1 cup sour cream

½ cup chopped onion

1 can (4½ ounce) chopped green chilies

1½ cups (6 ounces) fancy shredded Monterey Jack cheese

1 can (8-count) refrigerated Hill Country Fare Jumbo's™ Buttermilk Biscuits

The best ranch cooks know biscuits and beef are guaranteed to bring the cowboys galloping home when they hear the dinner bell. This dish is simple and hearty, with flaky biscuits surrounding a savory filling of spicy barbecued brisket, creamy cheeses and green chiles. Think of this creation as ranch-style comfort food!

1. Heat oven to 375°F. Spray a 9 x 13-inch baking dish with non-stick cooking spray.

2. Add half of sour cream (½ cup) to shredded brisket in container; stir to combine and set aside.

3. Combine remaining ½ cup sour cream, onion, green chilies and ¾ cup cheese.

4. Separate 4 biscuits into 8 halves; arrange biscuit halves over bottom of prepared dish. Spread BBQ beef mixture over biscuits; spread green chili-cheese mixture over beef. Separate remaining 4 biscuits into 8 halves and arrange over top.

5. Bake 20 minutes or until biscuits are lightly browned. Remove from oven and sprinkle with remaining ¾ cup cheese; return to oven 2 minutes longer or until cheese melts. Remove from oven, cut into squares and serve.

Serve BBQ Beef & Biscuit Casserole with Steamed Green Beans and Corn-on-the-Cob.

Beef and Penne with Sun-Dried Tomatoes

Preparation Time: 15 minutes
Cooking Time: 20 minutes
Makes 4 to 6 Servings

1 bag (12 ounce) frozen **H-E-B Fully Cooked® Beef Fajitas**

12 ounces penne rigate pasta (about 4 cups dry)

1 large onion

1 large red bell pepper, seeds and stem removed

2 cloves garlic, minced

8 to 10 large fresh basil leaves

1 jar (8 ounce) julienne cut sun-dried tomatoes in oil

½ cup shredded Parmesan cheese

When you can have a home cooked dinner on the table 30 minutes after you walk in the door at the end of a long day, that's a great meal! With H-E-B Fully Cooked® Beef Fajita strips this dish only tastes like you've slaved away in the kitchen all day. It's delicious piping hot, but just as good after standing at room temperature an hour, or even refrigerated for several hours—perfect for nights when dinner's in shifts because of busy family schedules.

1. Bring 3 quarts water to a boil in a 5-quart pot; cook pasta according to package directions. Drain and set aside.

2. Meanwhile, heat fajitas in microwave according to package directions. Cut onion and bell pepper in half, then into thin strips. Mince garlic. Remove basil leaves from stems; stack leaves and cut into very thin slices.

3. Drain oil from tomatoes into a large skillet. Heat skillet over Medium heat 3 minutes. Add onion, bell pepper and garlic; sauté 8 to 10 minutes or until tender. Add tomatoes and fajitas to skillet. Stir occasionally to heat through, about 6 to 8 minutes.

4. Combine pasta with beef mixture in a large serving bowl. Toss with Parmesan, sprinkle with basil and serve.

Serve Beef & Penne with Sun-Dried Tomatoes with Hot French Bread.

Green Chili Chicken Enchiladas

Preparation Time: 10 minutes
Baking Time: 20 minutes
Makes 4 to 6 Servings

1 tub (12 ounce) **H-E-B Fully Cooked® Seasoned Shredded Chicken**

16 corn tortillas

2 cups (8 ounces) shredded cheddar Jack cheese, divided

1 can (14½ ounce) green enchilada sauce

Sour cream, for garnish, optional

If you are like a lot of Texans, the week isn't complete without at least one Mexican meal. Why not make this dish, with its green chile sauce in place of the traditional red, a regular in your South-of-the-Border repertoire? H-E-B has already cooked, seasoned, and shredded the chicken for you, so you'll have dinner on the table in no time flat.

1. Heat oven to 350°F. Spray a 9 x 13-inch baking dish with non-stick cooking spray.

2. Heat tortillas briefly in microwave. Pull chicken apart to "shred."

3. Reserve 1½ cups of enchilada sauce for topping and set aside. Pour remainder of sauce into a shallow bowl.

4. Dip 1 tortilla in sauce to coat both sides. Lay tortilla on flat surface. Place 2 to 3 tablespoons chicken down center of tortilla; top with 1 tablespoon cheese. Roll up tortilla and place in prepared baking dish, seam-side down.

5. Repeat step 4 with remaining tortillas. Pour 1½ cups reserved sauce over enchiladas and top with remaining cheese (about 1 cup).

6. Bake 20 minutes, uncovered, or until filling is hot and cheese melts and bubbles. Remove from oven and serve while hot. Top with sour cream, if desired.

Serve Green Chili Chicken Enchiladas with Refried Beans, Mexican Skillet Rice and Fresh Guacamole.

Beef and Vegetable Frittata

Preparation Time: 15 minutes
Baking Time: 15 minutes
Makes 4 to 6 Servings

1½ cups frozen **H-E-B Fully Cooked® Italian Beef Crumbles**

2 medium red potatoes, diced (2 cups)

1 small zucchini, chopped (1 cup)

1 small red bell pepper, seeds and stem removed

½ cup finely chopped onion

2 tablespoons olive oil

1 teaspoon **each** salt, black pepper and dried thyme leaves

4 ounces Gruyère cheese, shredded (1 cup)

6 large eggs, beaten

Frittatas are no-fuss omelets you make right in your old cast iron skillet. They're the perfect dish for ad libbing, as you can toss in whatever produce, meat, herbs and cheese you discover in your garden, market or refrigerator. This hearty frittata is perfect for a late night supper enjoyed in the comfort of your cozy kitchen and just as welcome for breakfast and brunch. Kids enjoy black olives sprinkled on top to give it the fun look of pizza.

1. Heat oven to 425°F. Position oven rack in top third of oven.

2. Dice potatoes into ½-inch pieces. Cut zucchini lengthwise into quarters, then crosswise into ¼-inch thick slices. Cut bell pepper into ¼-inch pieces. Chop onion finely.

3. Heat oil in a 12-inch oven-proof skillet over Medium-High heat. Sauté potatoes and onion in oil 5 minutes. Add zucchini, red pepper, salt, pepper and thyme; cook 5 more minutes. Stir in beef crumbles and remove from heat.

4. Shred cheese. Sprinkle cheese over beef-vegetable mixture in skillet. Beat eggs; pour evenly over top.

5. Bake frittata, uncovered, 15 minutes or until set (when top feels firm to the touch and knife inserted in center comes out clean). Remove from oven and let stand 5 minutes. Cut into wedges and serve while hot.

Serve Beef and Vegetable Frittata with Hot Biscuits and Tossed Mixed Greens or Fruit Salad.

Smoked Brisket with Portobello-Cranberry Sauce

Preparation Time: 20 minutes
Heating Time: 40 to 45 minutes
Makes 12 to 16 Servings

3 to 4 pounds **H-E-B Fully Cooked® Brisket Flat**

1 medium onion, chopped

4 cloves garlic, chopped

2 tablespoons chopped fresh rosemary

2 tablespoons butter

12 ounces sliced fresh portobella mushrooms

1 can (10½ ounce) condensed beef broth

1¼ cups dry red wine

⅔ cup frozen cranberry juice concentrate, thawed

¼ cup flour

1 cup (4 to 5 ounces) dried cranberries

Heavy-duty aluminum foil

When company is coming or you want a special family holiday dinner, pull out all the stops with this show-stopping, festive entrée. While it will look and taste amazing, only you will know how easy it was. Best of all, it won't keep you away from the festivities very long. In an hour from start to finish, you can get it in the oven and while it bakes prepare the side dishes and set the table.

1. Heat oven to 350°F.

2. Chop onion and garlic. Remove rosemary leaves from stems and chop.

3. Melt butter in a large skillet over Medium heat. Add onion, garlic, rosemary and mushrooms; sauté 5 to 7 minutes or until mushrooms are tender.

4. Blend beef broth, red wine, cranberry concentrate and flour in a 3-quart saucepan with a wire whisk. Stir mushroom mixture and dried cranberries into sauce. Bring to a boil; heat until thickened and remove from heat; stir frequently.

5. Meanwhile, trim fat from brisket; slice brisket across the grain into ¼-inch thick slices. Place a piece of heavy-duty foil large enough to wrap over the brisket on a large baking sheet. Place brisket on foil; separate slices slightly to pour sauce over and between slices. Seal foil tightly.

6. Heat brisket in oven 40 to 45 minutes until heated thoroughly. Transfer to a platter and serve while hot.

Serve Beef Brisket with Cranberries and Portobello Mushrooms with Potato Pancakes and Steamed Fresh Broccoli.

Beef and Ravioli Casserole

Preparation Time: 10 minutes
Baking Time: 45 to 50 minutes
Makes 6 to 8 Servings

1 bag (12 ounce) frozen
H-E-B Fully Cooked®
Italian Beef Crumbles

Non-stick cooking spray

1 box (10 ounce) frozen
chopped spinach, thawed

1 jar (26 ounce) puttanesca
pasta sauce

1 bag (30 ounce) frozen cheese-
filled ravioli

8 ounces (2 cups) shredded
mozzarella cheese

⅔ cup grated Parmesan cheese

What a creative idea! Your family and guests will love this recipe and you will, too. It tastes just like everyone's favorite lasagna, without all the work. Cheese-filled ravioli and seasoned cooked beef crumbles save you the hassle of cooking lasagna noodles, making a fancy cheese filling, and cooking the meat. In fact, you can have this ready to pop into the oven in 10 minutes.

1. Heat oven to 375°F. Spray a 9 x 13-inch baking dish with non-stick spray.

2. Squeeze thawed spinach thoroughly to remove moisture.

3. Spoon just enough pasta sauce into prepared baking dish to coat bottom. Arrange half of frozen ravioli into rows over sauce. Spread all of spinach and half of frozen beef crumbles over ravioli. Sprinkle with half of mozzarella and Parmesan cheeses.

4. Layer remaining ravioli and beef crumbles over cheeses. Pour remaining pasta sauce evenly over top. Sprinkle with remaining cheeses. Cover dish tightly with foil.

5. Bake 30 minutes. Remove foil and bake 15 to 20 minutes longer or until casserole is bubbly and ravioli is heated thoroughly. Let stand 5 minutes. Cut into squares and serve.

Serve Beef and Ravioli Casserole with a Tossed Green Salad and Garlic Bread.

Beef-Stuffed Spaghetti Squash

Preparation Time: 15 minutes
Cooking Time: 25 minutes
Makes 4 Servings

1 bag (12 ounce) frozen
H-E-B Fully Cooked®
Beef Fajitas

1 spaghetti squash
(2 to 3 pounds)

1 small onion, chopped

1 medium green bell pepper,
chopped

2 medium tomatoes, chopped

1 tablespoon olive oil

½ cup grated Parmesan cheese

Salt, ground black pepper and
garlic powder

Just as the football season gets rolling, a pale yellow football-shaped winter squash peaks at markets. Although it's a vegetable, once cooked, the inside magically transforms itself into strands of golden spaghetti. Even kids love eating this fun vegetable. It can be used in any favorite pasta recipe. This recipe is sure to become a favorite at your house, as it's hearty enough for Texas-size appetites.

1. Heat oven to 350°F.

2. Pierce squash in 4 places with the tip of a knife. Microwave on High power 8 to 10 minutes, turning every 3 to 4 minutes, until squash is tender when pierced with a fork. Chop onion, bell pepper and tomatoes while squash cooks.

3. Cut squash in half lengthwise; remove seeds and discard. Using a fork, pull squash from edges into strands resembling spaghetti.

4. Heat fajitas in microwave according to package directions; cut into bite-sized pieces.

5. Heat oil in a large skillet over Medium heat. Add onion and bell pepper; sauté 5 minutes. Add squash strands, fajitas and tomatoes; toss to combine. Season to taste with salt, pepper and garlic powder.

6. Place squash shells on a baking sheet, cut sides up; fill each with beef and squash mixture, divided evenly. Top with Parmesan cheese; bake 10 minutes or until cheese melts and browns lightly. Cut each half into 2 portions and serve.

Serve Beef-Stuffed Spaghetti Squash with a Veggie Lover's Salad and Hot Garlic Bread.

Beef Tortilla Stacks

Preparation Time: 15 minutes
Cooking Time: 12 to 15 minutes
Makes 2 Stacks, 2 to 3 Servings each

1 bag (12 ounce) frozen **H-E-B Fully Cooked® Beef Fajitas**

Non-stick cooking spray

1 can (15 ounce) black beans

1 can (11 ounce) corn kernels

1 can (4½ ounce) chopped green chilies

8 flour tortillas (6-inch)

1 can (15 ounce) enchilada sauce

8 ounces (2 cups) shredded Monterey Jack cheese

These aren't enchiladas, but they're not quesadillas, either. They're both! Four "stories" of tortillas are filled with Tex-Mex favorites: fajita beef, beans, corn, chilies, and sauce all held together with melted cheese. Keep your fork and plenty of napkins—these are deliciously messy.

1. Heat oven to 425°F. Spray a large baking sheet with non-stick spray.

2. Meanwhile, heat fajitas in microwave according to package directions. Cut or tear fajitas into bite-sized pieces.

3. Rinse and drain black beans. Drain corn. Combine beans, corn and green chilies in a medium bowl.

4. Lay 2 tortillas on prepared baking sheet about 4 inches apart.

5. Spread 3 tablespoons enchilada sauce over each tortilla. Spread about ¼ cup fajita pieces and a scant ¼ cup bean mixture over sauce on each. Sprinkle ¼ cup cheese over each top.

6. Lay a second tortilla over cheese on each stack, then repeat layering process in step #5 to make 4 complete layers of tortillas and toppings, ending with remaining toppings.

7. Bake 12 to 15 minutes or until tortillas are browned and cheese melts. Cut into wedges and serve while hot.

Serve Beef Tortilla Stacks with Mexican Rice and Fresh Berries with Whipped Topping.

Mexican-Style Beef Stroganoff

Preparation Time: 10 minutes
Cooking Time: 20 minutes
Makes 4 Servings

1 bag (12 ounce) frozen **H-E-B**
Fully Cooked® Beef Fajitas

Non-stick cooking spray

1 onion, chopped

2 small zucchini squash, diced

1 tablespoon oil

½ cup beef broth

1 teaspoon cornstarch

1 cup prepared chipotle salsa

1 cup frozen corn kernels

1 cup (8 ounce) sour cream

Beef Stroganoff is a timeless family favorite. But it's fun to mix-up classic dishes with a seasonal or regional twist. To take beef stroganoff South-of-the-Border, we've swapped fideo for traditional wide egg noodles, added some favorite vegetables, and spiced up the traditional creamy sauce with a smokey chipotle salsa. It's time to start a new family tradition!

1. Heat fajitas according to package directions. Cut into bite-sized pieces.

2. Meanwhile, chop onion. Cut squash lengthwise into quarters, then cut into ¼-inch thick slices. Heat oil in a large skillet over Medium-High heat. Sauté onion and squash 5 to 7 minutes, or until tender.

3. Combine broth and cornstarch. Add broth mixture, fajitas, salsa and corn to skillet; cook 2 minutes or until hot and thickened slightly. Stir in sour cream and heat 5 more minutes. Remove from heat and serve while hot.

Serve Mexican-Style Beef Stroganoff over Fideo Vermicelli with a Tossed Salad and Hot Tortillas.

Skillet Pork with Sweet Potatoes and Apples

Preparation Time: 10 minutes
Cooking Time: 20 minutes
Makes 4 Servings

4 pieces frozen **H-E-B Fully Cooked® Black Pepper Glazed Bone-In Pork Chops**

1 large or 2 small sweet potatoes (about 1 pound)

1 medium onion

2 medium tart red apples

2 tablespoons butter

¼ teaspoon **each** salt, pepper and ground cinnamon

½ cup fresh orange juice

Make dinner a feast for the senses. The natural sweetness and rich autumn colors of sweet potatoes, apples and orange juice make this dish a favorite for fall evenings.

1. Peel sweet potatoes and cut crosswise into ¼-inch thick slices; stack slices and cut into quarters. Chop onion coarsely. Core apples. Cut into wedges; cut wedges in half, crosswise.

2. Melt butter in a large, deep skillet over Medium heat. Add potato and onion; sauté 6 to 8 minutes.

3. Stir in apples; sprinkle with salt, pepper and cinnamon; toss to coat. Pour in orange juice; lay frozen pork chops over top.

4. Cover skillet; reduce heat to Low and simmer 15 minutes or until potatoes are done and chops are heated thoroughly. Serve while hot.

Serve Skillet Pork with Sweet Potatoes and Apples with Steamed Broccoli.

Philly Beef, Spinach and Cheese Casserole

Preparation Time: 10 minutes
Baking Time: 20 to 25 minutes
Makes 6 Servings

1 bag (16 ounce) frozen
H-E-B Fully Cooked®
Sliced Philly Beef Steak

1 box (10 ounce) frozen
chopped spinach, thawed

4 ounces (½ cup) cream
cheese, softened

⅓ cup sour cream

¼ cup **plus** 2 tablespoons
grated Parmesan cheese

1½ cups pasta sauce with olives

1 cup (4 ounces) shredded
mozzarella cheese

1 can (8 ounce) refrigerated
Pillsbury® Crescent Rolls

*Tell the kids this is upside down, inside out lasagna they'll love it! You
will, too, as it takes just 10 minutes of effort and is guaranteed to win
over the hearts and tummies of your loved ones.*

1. Heat oven to 375°F. Heat Philly steak in microwave according to
package directions.

2. Meanwhile, squeeze spinach tightly to remove excess moisture.
Blend cream cheese and sour cream in a medium bowl; stir in
spinach and ¼ cup Parmesan. Spread spinach mixture evenly over
the bottom of a 9 x 13-inch baking dish.

3. Drain juices from beef. Combine beef with pasta sauce; spread
evenly over spinach mixture. Sprinkle with mozzarella cheese.

4. Unroll dough; lay over top of casserole and sprinkle with 2 tablespoons Parmesan. Bake 20 to 25 minutes or until top is golden
brown and casserole is heated thoroughly.

*Serve Philly Beef, Spinach and Cheese Casserole with a Mixed Green
Salad with Tomatoes and Cucumbers.*

Weeknight Beef Stroganoff

Preparation Time: 10 minutes
Cooking Time: 10 minutes
Makes 4 to 6 Servings

1 package (about 1½ pounds)
**H-E-B Fully Cooked® Beef
Pot Roast with Gravy**

1 tablespoon oil

1 onion, chopped

8 ounces sliced mushrooms

1 cup sour cream

Salt and coarse ground
black pepper

Classic Russian beef stroganoff is made with tender cuts of meat such as tenderloin tips or top loin, stirred into sautéed onions and mushrooms with beefy, sour cream gravy. It's as rich and meaty as dinner gets. H-E-B has made stroganoff a weeknight possibility when you start with (believe it or not) beef fully cooked until completely tender in its own rich gravy. You add your own special touch for a fresh, delicious meal that comes together in minutes. Your family will agree this is the best stroganoff they've ever tasted.

1. Heat oil in a large skillet over Medium-High heat. Add onion and mushrooms; sauté 5 minutes or until onion is tender.

2. Open pot roast package and empty gravy from roast package into skillet with onion and mushrooms. Stir to combine. Reduce heat to Medium-Low and simmer 5 minutes.

3. Meanwhile, cut pot roast into ½-inch thick slices; stack slices and cut into ½-inch thick strips.

4. Stir strips into skillet mixture; cover skillet and heat 5 minutes or until roast is hot. Stir in sour cream; season to taste with salt and pepper. Serve while hot.

Serve Weeknight Beef Stroganoff over Wide Egg Noodles with Steamed Baby Carrots and Hot French Bread.

Pork and Hominy with Corn Dumplings

Preparation Time: 10 minutes
Baking Time: 20 minutes
Makes 4 Servings

1 tub (16 ounce) **H-E-B Fully Cooked® Carne de Puerco, Seasoned Pork with Juices**

1 can (16 ounce) yellow hominy, drained

1 can (10 ounce) diced tomatoes with green chilies, drained

1 can (2¼ ounce) sliced black olives, drained

1 cup (4 ounces) shredded colby Jack cheese

1 tube (11½ ounce) refrigerated Pillsbury Cornbread Twists

Chopped cilantro or sliced green onions tops, optional, for garnish

Among Spanish families in New Mexico and Mexican families on both sides of the Rio Grande, a favorite family meal is pozole: lime-treated corn similar to hominy, stewed with pork and chiles, served with tortillas. Posole corn delightfully "pops" when it's cooked, becoming little chewy flowers with an intense corn-flavor. The corn also finds its way into many of the Mexican caldillos we love. The warmth of these spicy, long-simmering meaty stews is especially welcome when the weather turns cold. This chunky version cooks in just minutes and is topped with fun cornbread pinwheels.

1. Heat oven to 400F°.

2. Meanwhile, heat pork in microwave or on stovetop according to package directions; stir and break up pork cubes with edge of spoon. Drain hominy, tomatoes and olives; toss with pork. Spread mixture evenly in a 9-inch round baking dish or pie pan; sprinkle with cheese.

3. Open tube of cornbread twists. Do not unroll dough; separate at perforations into 8 rolls. Lay rolls over top of casserole, pinwheel-style; arrange 7 in a circle and 1 in the center.

4. Bake casserole 6 to 8 minutes or until tops of corn rolls just begin to brown; turn corn rolls over and bake casserole 15 minutes longer. Garnish with chopped cilantro or sliced green onion tops, if desired.

Serve Pork & Hominy with Corn Dumplings with Pear Wedges and Red Seedless Grapes.

Pot Roast and Mashed Potato Casserole

Preparation Time: 10 minutes
Cooking Time: 20 minutes
Makes 4 to 6 Servings

1 tub (16 ounce) **H-E-B Fully Cooked® Shredded Beef Pot Roast with Gravy**

1 package (16 ounce) frozen French-cut green beans

1 bag (20 ounce) refrigerated Simply Potatoes®, Country Mashed

¼ cup milk

½ teaspoon **each** salt and pepper

1 can (4 ounce) sliced mushrooms, drained

1 can (10½ ounce) cream of mushroom soup

1 can (2.8 ounce) French-fried onions

Aluminum foil

When life feels stressful or the weather outside turns harsh and cold, we yearn to come home to familiar, comforting foods. Forget salads or take-out. We want home cooked dishes from our childhood, things as reassuring as Grandma's hug and as cozy as an old shirt. Comfort foods vary from family to family, but for many of us it's pot roast with mashed potatoes and gravy. Here's the full meal in one dish.

1. Heat oven to 400°F.

2. Microwave pot roast according to package directions; break up any large pieces.

3. Meanwhile, place frozen green beans in a colander. Rinse with cool water to thaw. Squeeze beans thoroughly to drain excess moisture.

4. Microwave mashed potatoes according to package directions. Stir milk, salt and pepper into heated potatoes.

5. While potatoes heat, spread pot roast with gravy over bottom of a 9 x 13-inch baking dish. Layer green beans and mushrooms over roast. Spread mushroom soup over beans and mushrooms. Spread potatoes over soup. Top with French fried onions.

6. Cover loosely with foil and bake 20 minutes. Serve while hot.

Serve Pot Roast & Mashed Potato Casserole with Sliced Tomatoes and Dinner Rolls.

Pork Chops with Sweet and Sour Cabbage

Preparation Time: 10 minutes
Cooking Time: 35 minutes
Makes 4 to 6 Servings

4 pieces frozen **H-E-B Fully Cooked® Black Pepper Glazed Bone-In Pork Chops**

1 small head red cabbage, shredded (8 to 10 cups)

4 tablespoons butter

⅓ cup sugar

½ cup balsamic vinegar

¼ teaspoon **each** salt and pepper, or to taste

Here in central Texas, German and Czech specialties abound. Sweet-and-sour cabbage is a special favorite in many of our kitchens. Pork chops tend to pair up perfectly with many cabbage recipes and this one is no exception. In this case, you save precious time by using Fully Cooked® pork chops perfectly seasoned with a black pepper glaze.

1. Remove and discard outer leaves from cabbage. Cut cabbage in half and remove core. Slice cabbage as thinly as possible to "shred".

2. Melt butter in a large, deep skillet or 4-quart pot over Medium heat. Sauté cabbage in butter 5 to 7 minutes, until cabbage begins to wilt. Add sugar, vinegar, salt and pepper; toss to coat.

3. Reduce heat to Medium-Low; cover pot and simmer 15 minutes, stirring occasionally.

4. Lay frozen pork chops over top of cabbage. Cover pot; cook 15 minutes longer or until pork chops are heated thoroughly and cabbage is tender. Serve hot.

Serve Pork Chops with Sweet & Sour Cabbage with Buttered Noodles.

Calabacita con Puerco

Preparation Time: 10 minutes
Cooking Time: 25 to 30 minutes
Makes 4 to 6 Servings

1 tub (16 ounce) **H-E-B Fully Cooked® Carne De Puerco, Seasoned Pork with Juices**

2 pounds zucchini or tatuma squash (about 3 medium)

1 medium onion, coarsely chopped

1 tablespoon oil

1 teaspoon dried oregano leaves

1 can (14½ ounce) diced tomatoes

1 can (8 ounce) tomato sauce

1 can (11 ounce) corn kernels, drained

When the Spaniards came to the New World, they found that Indian cooking used variations of their basic staples: maize, beans and squash. Calabacitas (Spanish for "little squash") evolved from these Indian roots in the Southwest and it remains a popular side for nearly any Mexican food dish. We've taken this regional favorite and made it a meal with the addition of seasoned pork. Pass sour cream and fresh cilantro to complete the meal.

1. Wash squash; trim and discard ends; cut into ½-inch cubes. Chop onion coarsely.

2. Heat oil in a 5 or 6-quart pot over Medium-High heat 2 minutes. Add onion and zucchini; sauté 5 minutes. Stir in oregano. Reduce heat to Medium; stir and cook 5 more minutes.

3. Add pork with juices, tomatoes and tomato sauce; stir. Bring to a boil. Cover pot; reduce heat to Medium-Low. Cook 10 to 15 minutes or until pork is hot and vegetables are tender.

4. Stir in corn and cook 5 minutes longer, uncovered. Serve hot.

Serve Calabacita con Puerco with Hot Cornbread.

Beef and Green Chili Enchilada Casserole

Preparation Time: 15 minutes
Baking Time: 40 to 45 minutes
Makes 4 to 6 Servings

1 tub (12 ounce) **H-E-B**
Fully Cooked® Seasoned
Shredded Beef

12 corn tortillas

1 red bell pepper, seeds and
stem removed

1 can (15 ounce) black beans

12 ounces queso quesadilla
slices

1 can (7 ounce) chopped
green chilies

Sauce:

1 can (10 ounce) green chile
enchilada sauce

1 can (7 ounce) green
Mexican sauce

Texas is beef country and beef enchiladas are customary around these parts. This casserole is easy because it's "stacked" rather than rolled enchiladas, and it's made even easier when you start with the Fully Cooked® shredded beef. Enjoy the textures of the ingredients along with the delicious spiciness from the green chile! Serve with a spoonful of sour cream or Crema Mexicana, if you like, for the traditional cooling reme-dy for chile heat.

1. Heat oven to 350°F. Spray a 7 x 11-inch baking dish or 2-quart casserole with non-stick cooking spray.

2. Heat beef in microwave according to package directions. Separate beef shreds with 2 forks.

3. Meanwhile, tear tortillas into bite-sized pieces or chop coarsely. Chop bell pepper. Rinse and drain black beans. Separate cheese slices. Combine sauce ingredients.

4. To assemble casserole, spread half of tortilla pieces over bottom of prepared dish. Place half of beef shreds evenly over tortillas; layer half of bell pepper, half of black beans and half of green chilies over beef. Pour 1 cup sauce evenly over top. Lay half the cheese slices over sauce in a single layer.

5. Layer remaining ingredients in the same order listed in step #4.

6. Bake 40 to 45 minutes or cheese is browned around the edges and casserole is bubbly. Remove from oven and let stand 5 to 10 minutes. Cut into squares and serve while hot.

Serve Beef & Green Chili Enchilada Casserole with Fresh Express® Baby Spinach Trio Tossed with Mango Salad Dressing.

Chicken and Gnocchi Gorgonzola

Preparation Time: 10 minutes
Cooking Time: 10 minutes
Makes 4 Servings

2 pieces frozen **H-E-B Fully Cooked® Italian Seasoned Chicken Breasts**

1 pound gnocchi pasta

½ cup julienne sliced sun-dried tomatoes in oil, undrained

¼ cup pine nuts

¾ cup canned low-sodium or regular chicken broth

1 cup (4 ounces) crumbled Gorgonzola cheese

½ cup thinly sliced fresh basil leaves

Gnocchi are fun, light little pasta dumplings made of semolina, potatoes or spinach and ricotta. They can be found fresh, frozen or dried and cook like pasta, only faster. Chefs in Italy, where gnocchi are traditional, serve them with buttery tomato or creamy Gorgonzola sauces. We've combined the best of both in this rich creamy sauce, redolent with pine nuts, marinated dried tomatoes and Italian-seasoned chicken. Although this entrée goes together in minutes, it's special enough for the most discriminating palate.

1. Bring 4 quarts water to a boil in a 6-quart pot over High heat to cook gnocchi.

2. Meanwhile, heat chicken in microwave according to package directions. Cut chicken into bite-sized pieces.

3. Remove gnocchi from package and drop into boiling water. Cook 3 to 4 minutes or until gnocchi float to the top. Drain and set aside.

4. While gnocchi cooks, place tomatoes (undrained) and pine nuts in a large skillet over Medium heat. Sauté 3 to 4 minutes or until nuts are lightly browned. Add chicken broth and cheese; stir until cheese melts.

5. Add chicken, gnocchi and basil; stir and heat 2 more minutes or until mixture simmers.

Serve Chicken and Gnocchi Gorgonzola with a Tossed Italian Salad.

Weeknight Chicken Cacciatore

Preparation Time: 10 minutes
Cooking Time: 20 minutes
Makes 4 to 6 Servings

6 pieces frozen **H-E-B Fully Cooked® Herb Roasted Chicken Thighs**

1 onion, chopped

1 green bell pepper, seeds and stem removed

½ cup coarsely chopped pitted kalamata olives

2 tablespoons olive oil

8 ounces sliced fresh mushrooms

½ cup dry red wine or chicken broth

1 jar (26 ounce) marinara or pasta sauce

Salt and ground black pepper, to taste

American housewives made this dish one for the memory cookbook for many of today's baby boomers. It's even better than ever with herb-roasted chicken, fully-cooked to shorten cooking time.

1. Chop onion and bell pepper. Chop olives coarsely and set aside separately. Heat oil in a large, deep skillet or 4-quart pot. Sauté onion, bell pepper and mushrooms 6 to 8 minutes or until tender.

2. Add wine or broth; cook 30 to 60 seconds. Stir to loosen and combine any browned bits left in bottom of pot. Place frozen chicken in pot in a single layer, meat-sides down.

3. Add pasta sauce and olives; bring to a boil. Reduce heat to Medium-Low; cover and simmer 10 to 15 minutes or until chicken is heated thoroughly. Stir occasionally. Season to taste with salt and pepper. Serve while hot.

Serve Weeknight Chicken Cacciatore over Fettuccine with a Tossed Salad and Bread Sticks.

Pesto Chicken over Polenta

Preparation Time: 15 minutes
Cooking Time: 20 minutes
Makes 4 Servings

2 pieces frozen **H-E-B Fully Cooked® Pesto Seasoned Chicken Breasts**

2 ounces sun-dried tomatoes (dry, not packed in oil)

1 cup white wine

1 medium onion, chopped

1 tablespoon olive oil

Polenta:

1 can (14½ ounce) chicken broth

1½ cups water

¼ teaspoon salt

1 cup dry polenta or stone-ground cornmeal

½ cup cream or milk

⅓ cup shredded Asiago cheese

For centuries, Americans from the Southwest to Midwest have shared a love of cornmeal mush. It's the ultimate comfort food—rich and creamy spooned right from the pot or with a delightful crunchy exterior when fried or broiled. Today, we've given it gourmet status by calling it by its Italian name: polenta. This recipe combines the satisfying flavor and texture of polenta with tender, flavorful chicken breasts and rich, tangy sun-dried tomatoes.

1. For polenta, bring broth, water and salt to a boil in a 2-quart pot. Gradually stir in polenta or cornmeal; reduce heat to Low and cook 20 minutes, stirring occasionally.

2. Meanwhile, heat chicken in microwave according to package directions. Cut tomatoes into very thin strips; place in wine to soften about 10 minutes. Chop onion.

3. Heat oil in a large skillet over Medium heat. Sauté onion 6 to 8 minutes or until tender. Add tomatoes with wine and stir. Cook 30 to 60 seconds longer or until liquid has reduced by one-half. Remove from heat; cover skillet to keep warm.

4. Stir cream (or milk) and cheese into cooked polenta; remove from heat.

5. Slice chicken breasts thinly. Spoon polenta onto a serving platter or individual plates; lay chicken strips over polenta and top with onion-tomato mixture, including juices. Serve immediately.

Serve Pesto Chicken over Polenta with a Tossed Green Salad and Ciabatta Bread.

Chicken Pie Florentine

Preparation Time: 15 minutes
Cooking Time: 25 minutes
Makes 4 to 6 Servings

2 to 3 pieces frozen **H-E-B Fully Cooked® Seasoned Chicken Breasts**

1 package (15 ounce, two 9-inch) refrigerated pie crusts

1 package (10 ounce) frozen chopped spinach, thawed

½ medium onion, chopped

1¼ cups prepared Alfredo sauce

¼ teaspoon each salt and ground black pepper

⅛ teaspoon ground nutmeg

The classic marriage of a creamy sauce and spinach—"a la Florentine" (meaning in the style of cooks in Florence, Italy)—is even better with a flavor and protein boost from seasoned chicken breasts and when everything is tucked into a delicate pastry. It's almost sinful how easy and delicious this is. Cut into pie-shape pieces and serve with a simple salad for an elegant luncheon or dinner entrée.

1. Heat oven to 400°F. Bring pie crusts to room temperature according to package directions.

2. Meanwhile, heat chicken in microwave according to package directions. Squeeze spinach thoroughly to drain. Chop onion.

3. Unfold one pie crust and place in ungreased 9-inch glass pie pan. If crust cracks, wet fingers and push together to seal. Press crust firmly against sides and bottom of pan; trim crust at pan edge. Prick bottom and sides of crust with a fork about 20 times. Bake crust 5 to 7 minutes, until a light golden brown.

4. While crust bakes, dice chicken into ½-inch cubes; combine chicken and onion with ½ cup Alfredo sauce in a medium bowl. Blend spinach, remaining ¾ cup Alfredo sauce, salt, pepper and nutmeg in a separate bowl.

5. Spoon chicken mixture into crust. Spread spinach mixture evenly over chicken mixture. Unfold remaining crust and place over top. Fold back edges of crust and squeeze or crimp with fingers to stand up at outer edge of pan. Cut 4 slits in top crust.

6. Bake 20 minutes or until crust is browned on top and filling is hot. Let stand 5 minutes, cut into wedges and serve.

Serve Chicken Pie Florentine with a Tossed Green Salad.

Szechwan Chicken and Vegetable Stir Fry

Preparation Time: 5 minutes
Cooking Time: 10 minutes
Makes 4 Servings

½ bag (11 ounces or 10 to 12 pieces) frozen **H-E-B Fully Cooked® Szechwan Chicken**

1 bag (12 to 16 ounces) fresh vegetables for stir fry

1 tablespoon vegetable oil

1 cup **plus** 2 tablespoons canned chicken broth

¼ cup hoisin sauce

1 tablespoon soy sauce

2 teaspoons cornstarch

1 teaspoon sesame oil

Dishes from the Szechwan region of China are famous for their skillful use of a wide range of hot and peppery spices. Most distinctive is the mild, fragrant Szechwan peppercorn used in many dishes. Szechwan's characteristic style of stir-frying precooks meat in lots of oil. Using H-E-B's Fully Cooked® Szechwan chicken lets you achieve similar results with a lot less fat or fuss.

1. Heat chicken in microwave according to package directions.

2. Meanwhile, heat a large, non-stick skillet or wok over Medium-High heat 3 minutes. Add oil and tilt to coat pan. Add vegetables; stir-fry 3 to 5 minutes, until just crisp-tender. Remove to a bowl and cover to keep warm.

3. Pour 1 cup broth, hoisin sauce and soy sauce into skillet or wok; stir and bring to a boil. Add chicken; reduce heat to Medium and simmer 2 minutes.

4. Dissolve cornstarch in 2 tablespoons broth. Add cornstarch solution and sesame oil to skillet; stir to blend until sauce thickens. Add vegetables back to skillet; toss to coat. Serve hot.

Serve Szechwan Chicken & Vegetable Stir Fry over Steamed Rice or Chinese Noodles.

Chuckwagon Chicken Skillet

Preparation Time: 5 minutes
Cooking Time: 15 minutes
Makes 4 Servings

1 bag (12 ounce) frozen
**H-E-B Fully Cooked® Chicken
Breast or Thigh Fajitas**

1 can (10 ounce) Rotel®
Festival Diced Tomatoes with
Lime Juice and Cilantro

¾ cup water

1½ cups frozen Chuckwagon
Corn

1 can (15 ounce) black beans,
rinsed and drained

1 box (6 ounce) Uncle Ben's®
Mexican Fiesta Rice mix

1 cup (4 ounces) shredded
cheddar Jack jalapeño cheese

On trail drives over a century ago, chuck wagon cooks used their skillets for just about everything. Home cooks today are no different. We still love the convenience of skillet dinners that let us cook and serve everything from one pan. In this delightfully seasoned one-pan meal, we've blended the distinctive flavor combinations of tomatoes, lime, and cilantro with black beans, rice and chicken fajitas to create a speedy Southwestern pièce de résistance. Your family will wonder how they could ever "git along" without it.

1. Combine tomatoes with juice, water, corn and black beans in a large, deep skillet. Bring to a boil over Medium-High heat. Stir in rice and contents of seasoning packet.

2. Reduce heat to Low and cover skillet tightly. Simmer 10 minutes or until most of the liquid has absorbed; stir. Remove skillet from heat.

3. While rice cooks, microwave chicken according to package directions.

4. Arrange chicken over cooked rice mixture; sprinkle with cheese. Cover and let stand 5 minutes or until cheese melts. Serve while hot.

Serve Chuckwagon Chicken Skillet with Warm Flour or Corn Tortillas.

Mediterranean Chicken Pasta

Preparation Time: 10 minutes
Cooking Time: 10 minutes
Makes 4 Servings

12 ounces (½ bag) frozen
**H-E-B Fully Cooked® Breaded
Chicken Breast Chunks**

12 ounces (2 cups) uncooked
orecchiette pasta

1 tomato, diced

½ cup chopped green onions,
including tops

¼ cup chopped kalamata olives

½ cup shredded Romano cheese

Dressing:

2 tablespoons olive oil

1 tablespoon fresh lemon juice

¼ teaspoon coarse ground
black pepper

If you are a fan of Italian food, you've no doubt fallen in love with chicken that's roasted with lemon, salt and black pepper. That's it— simple, but perfect. The chicken comes out tender with a delectable crisp crust and lemony juices. Thus the inspiration for this equally simple pasta recipe highlighting chunks of crispy breaded chicken breast, a lemony dressing, and a beloved fresh pasta.

1. Bring 3 quarts water to a boil in a 5-quart pot. Cook pasta in boiling water according to package directions. Drain well.

2. Meanwhile, heat chicken in microwave according to package directions. Cut chicken chunks into quarters; set aside and cover to keep warm.

3. Dice tomato. Chop green onions, including tops. Chop olives.

4. Whisk dressing ingredients together in a large serving bowl. Add hot, drained pasta and toss to coat. Add chicken chunks, tomato, green onions, olives and cheese. Toss to combine and serve warm.

Serve Mediterranean Chicken Pasta with a Tossed Italian Salad and Hot Garlic Bread.

Side Dishes

Sweet and Sour Coleslaw

Preparation Time: 10 minutes
Makes 6 to 8 Servings

1 bag (16 ounce) refrigerated coleslaw

1 yellow, orange or red bell pepper, seeds and stem removed

½ small red onion

2 cups shredded or julienne-cut carrots

½ cup golden raisins

Dressing:

⅓ cup apple cider vinegar

3 tablespoons honey

2 tablespoons vegetable oil

2 teaspoons fresh lemon juice

½ teaspoon each salt and pepper

There are probably as many variations of coleslaw—from the Dutch kool ("cabbage") plus sla ("salad")—as there are bluebonnets in the Hill Country. This version begs to be served at a picnic by the lake, but it's a fine accompaniment to savory pork or poultry suppers at home, too.

1. Cut bell pepper and onion into ¼-inch thick strips.

2. Whisk dressing ingredients together in a medium bowl.

3. Toss coleslaw, bell pepper, onion, carrots and raisins with dressing in a large bowl. Cover and chill 30 minutes before serving, if time permits.

Corn and Green Chilies

Preparation Time: 5 minutes
Cooking Time: 10 minutes
Makes 4 Servings

1 tablespoon butter

1 can (7 ounce) diced green chilies

½ cup chopped onion

1 bag (16 ounce) frozen corn kernels

½ cup shredded Monterey Jack cheese

½ cup sour cream

Salt and ground black pepper, to taste

There are more than 200 varieties of chilies, more than 100 of which are indigenous to Mexico. For those of us who share with our southern neighbors a love of these pungent pods, that means incorporating them into mealtimes as often as possible. Combined with cheese, sour cream, and onions, plus the world's most versatile vegetable—corn—green chilies add mild fire to an already warm and satisfying dish.

1. Melt butter in a large skillet over Medium heat. Sauté chilies and onion in butter 3 minutes.

2. Add corn and cheese; stir and heat 5 minutes or until corn is hot and cheese melts.

3. Stir in sour cream just before serving. Season to taste with salt and pepper. Serve hot.

Chipotle-Cheese Mashed Potatoes

Preparation Time: 10 minutes
Cooking Time: 10 minutes
Makes 4 Servings

1 package (20 ounce) Simply Potatoes®, Country Mashed

2 to 3 individual canned chipotle peppers in adobo sauce, finely chopped

4 ounces white cheddar cheese, shredded (1 cup)

3 tablespoons butter

2 to 4 tablespoons milk

Salt and white ground pepper, to taste

When potatoes were first introduced to Europe in the late 16th century, people feared they were deadly. South America's Incas knew better, however. They had been cultivating the tubers for thousands of years. Needless to say, potatoes eventually caught on, and today in this country, they are the quintessential comfort food. This piquant take on a gold standard uses already mashed potatoes to brilliant effect. Stir in chipotle chiles in adobo sauce, and in a flash, you've got a smashing accompaniment to just about any Southwestern entree.

1. Finely chop 2 or 3 chipotle peppers, according to taste preference. Shred cheese and set aside.

2. Melt butter in a 3-quart saucepan over Medium heat. Add potatoes, chipotle peppers and 2 tablespoons milk. Heat thoroughly and stir frequently.

3. Add cheese; stir until melted. If potatoes are too thick, add 1 to 2 tablespoons additional milk to reach desired consistency. Serve while hot.

Mexican Skillet Rice

Preparation Time: 10 minutes
Cooking Time: 30 minutes
Makes 4 to 6 Servings

1 cup chopped yellow or
white onion

1 small bell pepper, seeds
and stem removed

4 cloves garlic, minced

1½ tablespoons oil

1½ cups uncooked long-grain
white rice

1 can (10 ounce) diced
tomatoes and green chilies,
mild or hot

1 can (14½ ounce) chicken
broth

½ cup water

This one-pot dish, a true Texas staple, couldn't be easier. A blend of fresh bell pepper, onion, garlic, and green chilies gives the rice intense flavor and fragrance. If you have any leftovers, consider making a rice salad with bottled vinaigrette, feta cheese, and chopped fresh vegetables. Or stir cold rice into beaten eggs, heat in oven-proof skillet, and sprinkle the frittata with Parmesan. Any way you cook this adaptable side, you can't go wrong.

1. Chop onion and pepper; chop garlic very finely to mince.

2. Heat oil in a heavy, large skillet over Medium heat. Sauté onion, pepper and garlic 3 minutes. Add rice; sauté 5 minutes or until golden. Stir frequently.

3. Add tomatoes with green chilies, chicken broth and ½ cup water. Stir and bring to a boil; reduce heat to Low and cover skillet. Simmer 15 to 20 minutes or until liquid has absorbed. Remove from heat; let stand 5 minutes, fluff with a fork and serve.

Jicama and Citrus Salad

Preparation Time: 10 minutes
Makes 4 to 6 Servings

2 cups peeled and julienned jicama (see step 1)

2 large navel oranges, peel and white pith removed

1 red bell pepper, cut into thin strips, seeds and stem removed

2 tablespoons chopped fresh cilantro

2 tablespoons brown sugar

1 tablespoon fresh-squeezed lemon juice

Watercress or torn romaine lettuce, optional

In the gleaming culinary school kitchen upstairs at San Antonio's H-E-B Central Market, Latin American cooking is in the spotlight, and this salad could be one of its stars. Also called Mexican potato, crunchy jicama headlines this sideshow attraction. The bulbous root imparts its sweet, nutty character while fresh, local oranges and lemons play sweet and tangy supporting roles worthy of applause. You'll be praise-worthy, too, when you produce this cool, refreshing salad at your table.

1. Peel jicama. Cut into ¼-inch thick slices; stack slices and cut into ¼-inch wide x 2-inch long strips. Place in a medium bowl.

2. Remove peel and white pith from oranges with a sharp knife. Cut orange sections from between membranes into bowl with jicama; hold oranges over bowl to catch juice from oranges. Squeeze orange membranes into bowl for additional juice.

3. Add bell pepper, cilantro, brown sugar and lemon juice. Toss thoroughly. Let stand 5 to 10 minutes before serving or chill 30 minutes, if time permits. Serve salad over watercress or torn romaine leaves.

Mom's Potato Salad

Preparation Time: 15 minutes
Cooking Time: 20 to 30 minutes
Makes 6 to 8 Servings

2 to 3 pounds gold or white potatoes

3 hard-boiled eggs, peeled

½ cup finely chopped celery

¼ cup finely chopped dill pickle

Dressing;

¾ cup mayonnaise, regular or reduced-fat

2 teaspoons spicy brown or stone-ground mustard

1 teaspoon salt

½ teaspoon ground black pepper

An all-American necessity at summer get-togethers and reunions, this creamy, old-fashioned potato salad uses dill pickle, eggs, and mustard to complement the humble tubers. Its name says it all. Family and guests will be hard-pressed to pass this country-style dish to their right. They'll want it close at hand for comfort, just where Mom should be.

1. Scrub potatoes or peel, as desired; cut into ½-inch or bite-sized pieces. Place in a 6-quart pot, cover with water and bring to a boil. Cook over Medium heat 20 to 30 minutes or until tender, uncovered.

2. Drain potatoes in a colander; let stand 10 to 15 minutes to drain well and cool slightly.

3. Meanwhile, chop eggs, celery and pickle. Combine dressing ingredients in a small bowl.

4. Toss potatoes, eggs, celery and pickle in a large serving bowl. Add dressing; stir gently to coat. Serve salad warm or refrigerate and serve chilled.

Index